Andrew Simms is Policy Director of ~~nef~~ (the new economics foundation), an award winning UK ~~~~~~~~ ~~~~~~~~~~~. For several years he worked for international development charities and is on the board of Greenpeace UK. He has written extensively on the issues of climate change and poverty reduction. In a series of groundbreaking reports on 'Ghost Town Britain' and 'Clone Town Britain', Andrew coined new terms and changed the debate on the impact of mass retailing. He lives in London with his wife, daughter and bicycle. He is the author of *Ecological Debt* and *Tescopoly*.

Joe Smith is a writer and academic based at the Open University. He works to provoke new thinking on the political and cultural dimensions of environmental change. Joe has written books on the green movement, climate change and the media and sustainability. He has acted as consultant on major BBC environment-related projects. More strategic work has included organizing a regular forum for leading media decision-makers that has run since 1996. He is the initiator and director of the Interdependence Day project, a collaboration that currently includes the Open University, nef and Sheffield University. The project is playing with new approaches to researching and communicating global issues. Joe lives in Cambridge with his wife and three boys.

Praise for *Tescopoly*

'Very passionate, very well written, very well researched.'
Andrew Marr, *Start the Week*, BBC Radio 4

'Simms's work succeeds as activism as well as analysis. His gift for human stories as well as financial ones and his adept coinage of phrases and ideas that challenge Tesco's dominance should ensure that his message is widely heard.'
The Times

'A passionate, powerful polemic.' *Independent on Sunday*

'An eloquent and persuasive account of modern corporate greed, and how and why we should resist it ... should make all but the Gordon Geckos of this world determined to do something about it.' Hugh Fearnley-Whittingstall

'Terrific ... no one can read this book and ever think of supermarkets as benign and life enhancing again.' Rosie Boycott

'Simms shows the creeping, invading unsustainable world of the supershop, its tentacles strangling the life out of our communities. Read it.' John Bird, founder of *The Big Issue*

'This is a blistering analysis of Tesco's domination of our economy – an illuminating and thought provoking read that might inspire readers to head for their nearest farmers' market.' *Sunday Express*

DO GOOD LIVES HAVE TO COST THE EARTH?

Edited by Andrew Simms and Joe Smith

CONSTABLE · LONDON

Constable & Robinson Ltd
3 The Lanchesters
162 Fulham Palace Road
London W6 9ER
www.constablerobinson.com

First published in the UK by Constable,
an imprint of Constable & Robinson Ltd, 2008

A copy of the British Library Cataloguing in
Publication Data is available from the British Library.

ISBN 978-1-84529-643-8

Printed and bound in the EU

1 3 5 7 9 10 8 6 4 2

Mixed Sources
Product group from well-managed
forests and other controlled sources
www.fsc.org Cert no. TT-COC-2341
© 1996 Forest Stewardship Council

To my parents, June Simms and David Simms, who have both led good lives, and also gave one to me.

&

For Betty Smith and remembering Aileen Bradley.

Contents

Acknowledgements

The theme and direction of this book have been informed by the work of the Interdependence Day project. Thanks are due to the supporters of the various strands of that work including the Open University Geography Discipline, Social Sciences Faculty and Open Broadcast Unit, DEFRA's Climate Challenge Fund and the research councils ESRC and NERC who funded the Interdependence seminar series (RES-496-25-4015). Corrina Cordon helped enormously by managing the logistics of pulling the book together. Ruth Potts provided enthusiasm and creative suggestions. Victoria Johnson, Sam Thompson, Perry Walker and Samantha Walton also gave support. Becky Hardie at Constable & Robinson thought that the book was a good idea and therefore allowed it to happen. Andreas Campomar ushered it into production. Rachel Maybank and Scarlett Simms restrained themselves as Andrew Simms crouched over his keyboard. All the authors did this in aid of promoting the notion that we can, in fact, lead good lives that don't have to cost the earth. They didn't do it for the money, because there wasn't any. The whole book was produced, in fact, without recourse to fast cars, long-haul holidays or luxury hotels. Aspects of the theme of the book were developed along with our colleagues in the Centre for Well-Being at nef (the new economics foundation) including Nic Marks, its founder and a contributor to this book, Nicola Steuer and Saamah Abdallah.

Introduction

In the last four decades people in the UK have become vastly more wealthy, and yet no happier. At the same time, environmental problems, above all climate change, suggest that our lifestyles have potentially catastrophic consequences.

Now, there is talk of costs and challenges, of a need to give up our cherished consumer indulgences in response to global environmental crises. But this book is motivated by a very simple and powerful idea: that the way we have been approaching these problems is upside-down.

The contributors to this book don't follow the mournful pessimism with which environmentalists have been labelled. We argue that our individual and general well-being isn't well served by the resource-hungry path we've taken. In fact, tackling environmental problems gives us an extraordinary chance to pause and rethink the way we live. Facing up to current global challenges could, in fact, propel us towards much better ways of living. The message is that good lives don't have to cost the Earth. But first, the bad news.

The new era of interdependence

From the moment that an *Apollo 17* astronaut pressed the shutter on a large format Hasselblad camera to take the first fully lit image of Earth from space, floating, like a blue marble in the darkness, we have been forced to acknowledge that we are a single global community of people, plants and animals, sharing one atmosphere. The image made obvious the need to stick together. If things went wrong, people could now see that there was nowhere else to run to, and no one likely to come to our rescue.

New ways of measuring now reveal exactly how interdependent are the people, biosphere and nations of our planet. The latest figures tracking our consumption in the UK plot our dependence on the world beyond the nation's borders. Taking a typical calendar year and using a very conservative measure, the most recent calculation suggests that from 15 April each year the nation in effect stops relying on its own natural resources and starts to 'live off' the rest of the world.

We've called this our 'ecological debt day' – the day when we begin living beyond our national environmental means. Our resource-hungry lifestyles have pushed that day ever earlier in the year over the last four decades. In 1961 it was 9 July. By 1981 Britain's ecological debt day was reached almost two months earlier, on 14 May. If the whole world wanted to copy our levels of consumption, we would need the resources – food, water, fuel and other materials – of more than three planets like Earth.

No single country has to live entirely within its own environmental means, but the world as a whole does. And, at the moment, the world goes into 'ecological debt' in early October. By over-fishing the oceans and pouring more greenhouse gases into the atmosphere than ecosystems can safely remove, in effect we are racking up an enormous ecological debt. The big debtor nations are the wealthy countries who have invested ever more of the riches of our life-support system in lavish lifestyles. China is increasingly attacked because its pollution levels are rising. But people overlook two very important issues. First, per person, China's greenhouse gas emissions are a fraction of those in Europe and the United States.

Amazingly, for all our claims to global leadership, Europe is less carbon-efficient at delivering well-being to its own citizens today than it was over forty years ago.[1] Second, a large amount of China's burning of fossil fuels is explained by the fact that it is manufacturing things to be consumed in wealthy countries. In the weeks before Christmas 2006 a cargo ship called the *Emma Maersk*, staggeringly huge at 400 metres long, made its maiden voyage from China to Felixstowe in Suffolk. On board, that single ship (and its owners plan to build another seven just like it) carried around 45,000 tonnes of stuff for people to buy and consume over the festive period.

The responsibility for over-consumption, and its costs and consequences, are very unevenly spread around the world. Our over-use of the fossil fuels that drive climate change is the clearest case. For example, by the time a typical British family sits down to its evening meal on 3 January, they will already have been responsible for a volume of greenhouse gases being pumped into the global commons of the atmosphere equivalent to that produced by a similar sized Tanzanian family in a year.[2] Yet, not only is Africa more vulnerable to climate change, it also has far less capacity to adapt.[3] Over 300 million people in sub-Saharan Africa live on less than $1 per day.[4] To try to imagine what that level of income means in terms of someone's daily life, it is the rough equivalent of a person in the UK trying to support an extended family of thirty-six people while living on the minimum wage. So, when things go wrong, there is little to fall back on.

The burden that our lifestyles place upon ecosystems is felt in many other ways. Our changing tastes and expectations around food are particularly influential. Research reported in the journal *Science*, for example, showed that fish stocks had collapsed in nearly one-third of the world's sea fisheries. Add pollution and changes to the temperature of the sea linked to global warming, and a lethal cocktail is being poured into our oceans. At current rates of decline in marine biodiversity, the researchers warned that by 2050 there would be little left to fish from the seas, with enormous impacts for humanity.[5]

A world trade system that evolved in an era of cheap fuel also drives the problem. At the same time that political leaders are imploring their citizens to cut greenhouse gas emissions, there are ships, lorries and planes passing in the night carrying identical products between rich, industrialized countries. The polluting emissions from this trade go largely uncounted, and the contributions from international shipping and air travel fall outside the scope of the international agreement to control climate change. In 2006, the UK imported 586 tonnes of gingerbread, sweet biscuits, waffles and wafers, pleasing many happy sweet teeth. But we exported a nearly identical amount – 669 tonnes. In the same year, the UK exported 1,445 tonnes of sweets to Sweden, then imported 1,632 tonnes from the same country.[6] Those are just a few examples, but whether it's potatoes rumbling between the UK and Germany, or milk, cream or frozen, boneless chicken cuts, the economy is awash with ecologically wasteful trade.

Two imported commodities – soya and palm oil – are taken for granted in the UK and slip almost invisibly into countless products ranging from biscuits to ready meals. The stories of these products reveal some of the impacts of our high-consuming lifestyles, and the need to look through a lens of interdependence to understand our impact on the world.

In 2005, we imported 774,623 tonnes of soya into the UK, with around two-thirds of it coming from Brazil.[7] Much of it goes into animal feed to support our relatively new-found habit of having plenty of meat and dairy products in our daily diet. But soya production is one of the key pressures that, along with forest fires, drought, deforestation and climate change, could push the Amazon rainforest over a 'tipping point' towards a massive die-back. If that happens it could turn the rainforest from being a store of greenhouse gases into a major new source. This is one of the potential phenomena that climate scientists tell us could trigger 'runaway climate change'. Perversely, it's something known among scientists as 'positive feedback'. But, of course, it isn't positive at all.

So, to respond to climate change, while we need to think about many different issues, we also need to get into the habit of thinking about all the connections between them, and see the environmental system as a whole. For example, the growth of palms for oil to supply biodiesel (and lots of food products) to the European market is now the main cause of deforestation in Indonesia.[8] Paradoxically it adds to greenhouse gas emissions, and is also driving our close mammalian cousin the orang-utan to extinction in the wild. Because of deforestation and land drainage, every tonne of palm oil produced in south-east Asia results in up to 33 tonnes of CO_2 emissions – ten times as much as conventional petroleum.[9] In 2005, the UK imported 652,110 tonnes of palm oil into the UK,[10] well over half of which came from south-east Asia. Although it is hard to tell how much came from existing plantations, and how much as a consequence of forest clearance, rising demand will place increasing pressure on forests.

Hopes that technological fixes and short cuts such as biofuels will offer a 'get out of gaol free' card are misplaced. The efficiency gains that we have managed to achieve in the last two to three decades, for example in transport, have been far outstripped by the fact that we are driving further, with more cars, and heavier higher performance vehicles. In short, 'Our environment does not respond to miles per gallon, it responds to gallons.'[11]

Despite thirty years of sophisticated environmental campaigning, international agreements and the creation of new agencies and gadgets, human societies continue to rack up ever more ecological debt. In the process we push parts of our natural life-support system beyond its ability to repair itself. We are borrowing from the ecologial security of future societies in order to pay for a way of life that is failing to bring us satisfaction. The currently dominant notion of a 'good life' as one that enjoys a big burn of fossil fuel energy and a high turnover of consumer goods is hazardous and unfulfilling.

Having a clearer picture of the state of the planet and its inherent vulnerability helps to raise awareness. But it can leave people feeling helpless and doesn't automatically offer people simple or desirable alternative courses of action. Many might conclude that environmental degradation is an inevitable and unavoidable consequence of raising living standards. But take a sharp-eyed look at the phrase 'living standards', and you'll see that in many of the world's wealthy countries, including the UK, there is precious little correlation between increasing consumption and increasing happiness over the last few decades. And today, someone in the UK who is consuming massively above their fair and sustainable share of the Earth's resources is no more likely to be satisfied with life than someone who is living within our collective environmental means.[12]

What is a 'good life', and where can I get one?

> Of all the things that wisdom provides to help one live one's entire life in happiness, the greatest by far is friendship.
>
> Epicurus 341–270 BC

The pursuit of the good life is an ancient philosophical question. In ancient Greece Aristotle wrote of the importance of a life well lived, and contrary to comic modern re-interpretations this had nothing to do with hitting the bottle, but was more to do with meaning and purpose. Influential eighteenth-century philosopher Jeremy Bentham made goodness the slave of cold, utilitarian calculation when he introduced the notion that society should be organized to provide the greatest good for the greatest number. The psychologist Carl Jung talked about the need for an individual to 'become all that one can be'. In the middle of the twentieth century Abraham Maslow lent his name to one attempt to define a hierarchy of human needs. The highest order of need, he called 'self-actualization'. This included things like creativity, morality, spontaneity, and the ability to solve problems. A direct contemporary of Maslow, Carl Rogers, spoke of the 'fully functioning person'. But the question is returning with a vengeance now that more people are waking up to the down sides of consumerism, and to the fact that our fuzzy-but-real environmental limits demand greater moderation on the part of the world's wealthy if everyone in the world is to meet their basic material needs.

There are several increasingly well-known indicators that point towards your chances for a happy, long life. For example, after biology has done its work and you have inherited the likelihood of a relatively longer or shorter lifespan from your parents, your chance for happiness is strongly influenced by how you are brought up in your first few years of life. Your chance of a long life is powerfully conditioned by whether you are wealthy enough to meet your basic needs, and by things like the quality and accessibility of your country's health service. Beyond the point of meeting your basic needs, the influence of income on life satisfaction shrinks dramatically. Then, a much stronger force is the activities you fill your time with, your relationships, and the attitude with which you approach your days (more of this below). In terms of your environmental footprint, the internet is now awash with simple calculators that tell you how many planet's worth of resources it would take if the whole world were to live at your level of material consumption.

Of these three dimensions, life expectancy, life satisfaction, and environmental impact, it is the measurement and meaning of the middle one which has troubled thinkers most since recorded human civilization began. Take these two divergent contemporary assessments from people whose careers have been built on addressing the fundamental question: what is a 'good life', and how do I get one? First there is Daniel Gilbert, professor of psychology at Harvard University and author of *Stumbling on Happiness:*

> Everyone who has observed human behaviour for more than thirty seconds seems to have noticed that people are strongly, perhaps even primarily, perhaps even single mindedly, motivated to feel happy.[13]

But compare Gilbert's conclusion to that reached by author and philosopher Alain de Botton:

> There are few things that humans are more dedicated to than unhappiness. Had we been placed on Earth by a malign creator for the exclusive purpose of suffering, we would have good reason to congratulate ourselves on our enthusiastic response to the task.[14]

Although apparently in complete conflict, the explanation that emerges from new studies of economics, psychology and biology is that we have most likely been pointed towards, and looked in, the wrong places. It seems that both positions are correct. We *are* single-mindedly motivated to feel happy, but by assiduously searching for happiness down the wrong lanes and alleyways we create the impression of being dedicated to the very opposite. The confusion can begin even with the words used to describe our desired state.

Gilbert plots three ways in which we use the term 'happy'. One is a simple emotional state that could be no more than 'bovine contentment'. The second is derived from knowledge of a life lived with purpose, engagement and meaning,

Aristotle's '*Eudaimonia*', meaning literally 'good spirit'. The third way in which we use the term happy is to pass judgement. That is to say, for example, having watched a sports match in which our favoured team performed atrociously, lost and deserved to lose, to comment that 'I am happy that the best team won', even if it wasn't the team that we supported. What is meant here is that we judge the outcome, objectively, to have been right and just, even if it left us emotionally disappointed.

Our collective environmental crisis does not end debate about what the 'good life' is: on the contrary. We believe that global environmental changes driven by human activity, above all climate change and biodiversity loss, can only be addressed by asking again, 'what does it mean to lead a good life?' This is not to say that we are convinced there is only one way to lead a 'good life'. Rather, this book brings together a range of authors, from different backgrounds and perspectives, to consider how it might be possible for all people on the planet to live lives that are pleasurable, purposeful and just, without overspending our environmental budget.

Social science has turned recently to the task of measuring the sense in which we might consider ourselves happy. The economist Richard Layard summarizes what has been learned in his popular book *Happiness: Lessons from a New Science*.[15] Accordingly, the key factors for our sense of happiness, in descending order of importance, include the genetic cards dealt to you at birth together with the circumstances and quality of parenting you experience in your early years – these are thought to account for up to half of our general level of happiness – and then:

Family relationships and outlook on life: being in a long term, stable family unit gives people higher levels of life satisfaction than not being so. Any disruption to that unit, for example through divorce, is one of the most serious threats to individual well-being. People do bounce back after such upheavals, but not, on average, to their previous levels. The nature of your family upbringing and in particular the role of your parents, also exerts a strong influence over setting your 'background' level of well-being. Day-to-day, a person who is involved in issues and group activities, who expresses themselves freely and chooses to focus more on the positive aspects of experience, so called 'healthy thinking', will have a higher level of life satisfaction and fewer of a range of health problems. Having a positive outlook and higher level of life satisfaction predicts a range of health benefits including less risk of acute illnesses like heart attacks, less risk of chronic illnesses like diabetes, muscular and skeletal problems, and, indeed, a longer life.

Economic situation: this is the next most important condition. Income is closely related to life satisfaction but only up to the point that the basics of life are met. In rich countries (effects are relative as well as absolute), the link begins to break down when incomes pass roughly the $15,000 per year mark. A rise in income will typically deliver a short-lived fillip, but it soon wears off. A drop in income, however, does bring us down, although the effect is small compared to the ups and downs of family relationships.

Work is important too, but not primarily for the income it gives us. Work matters because it gives us two important things: social contact and, potentially, the sense of contributing to society – in other words, it brings meaning to our lives. Unemployment, by contrast, isolates us socially, robs us of a sense of purpose *and* reduces our incomes. For these reasons, and counter-intuitively, retirement can harm a person's well-being. But work doesn't have to take the form of conventional, paid office or factory work – it could just as effectively be voluntary or care work.

Community and friendships are also important. A strong sense of community, or a high level of 'social capital', is important because it is associated with high levels of trust. Levels of communal trust vary widely around the world; for example, levels of trust are much higher in Norway than they are in the US. In caricature, the more equal, cohesive and 'social' a country is, such as among the Scandinavian nations, the happier the people tend to be. Strongly market-led economies, on the other hand, tend to deliver greater inequality and lower levels of trust. And, as far as the concerns of this book go, such countries are also much less efficient at converting natural resources, through the economy, into long and happy lives.[16]

Health matters to our sense of well-being but, surprisingly, not as much as you might imagine. The secret is in our adaptability. What research shows is that if we fall ill, or have an accident, even if the latter leads to some kind of disability, we have a knack of 'bouncing back' to, or close to, our prior level of happiness.

Two other issues are significant in determining life satisfaction. First, the nature of *government* we live under, and the degree to which we consider ourselves to be in control of our own destinies. Having rights and personal freedom matter. People who have *belief systems* that lead them to more altruistic behaviour, and that put value on 'doing good' in the wider world are also generally happier. So, difficult as it may be in a self-obsessed consumer culture, if we can take a step out of ourselves to engage in doing something in which we, as individuals, are not the main focus, paradoxically our personal well-being is likely to improve.

From this list it becomes possible to see why levels of happiness vary widely around the world. Things like divorce and unemployment rates, strength of community, levels of trust and the quality and nature of our institutions will all affect the degree to which people feel happy.

Perhaps more surprising than this list is the parallel catalogue of attributes that don't seem to influence our levels of happiness. If we all knew that age, looks and intelligence make little difference to personal happiness we would perhaps worry (and envy) youth, beauty and smartness less – and become happier in the process. It seems that the American newsreader who famously tore up her script on-air, appalled that the lead story of the day concerned the foibles of a rich, beautiful, celebrity socialite (Paris Hilton), really did know what she was doing.

There are as many ways of interpreting and finding the exact balance of a good life as there are people. But we think it is fair to say that good lives contain (preferably all of) three elements. A good life is full of positive emotions – these can be thought of as emotions about the future (optimism, hope, confidence, trust), the present (pleasure, savouring, comfort, mindfulness, bliss) and the past (contentment, pride, satisfaction, serenity). The engaged life is full of interest and challenge – using your particular skills and strengths in dynamic activities. Thirdly, a meaningful life is one that is engaged in pursuits and interests that are in service of something beyond the individual self.

That brief summary of what makes us happy describes what is likely to give us the feeling of a 'good life'. It also helps us understand what will undo it. The other side of the coin is etched with the economic and social dead weights that drag the good life down. High divorce rates undermine families; insecure and poorly paid employment fractures social cohesion, and high crime rates erode trust.

Time spent with family, friends and in growing and maintaining communities is vital to our well-being. It matters to have time available for outwardly focused actions that carry social purpose. Beyond a certain level, income doesn't. More than that, the psychological dissatisfaction intrinsic to being trapped on the consumer treadmill means that materialism can make us feel worse. If we overwork ourselves in order to raise the income to afford to keep running on the treadmill, we have less time available for the things that really do make us feel good. The struggle for a shorter working week is an old one. Yet working less and sharing out the work that is available more seems to make sense. Work matters, helping to create a sense of belonging and purpose. But too much or none at all and the result becomes negative. Shorter working hours would create more time for things that generate lasting well-being: pursuing individual interests, family, friendships and community involvement. Indirectly, less income would also reduce over-consumption.

American writer Barbara Ehrenreich points out the irony that in fifteenth-century France one in every four days was an official holiday.[17] Compare that to France's modern struggle to protect its thirty-five hour, five day working week. 'Despite the reputation of what are commonly called "The Middle Ages" as a time of misery and fear', writes Ehrenreich, 'the period can be seen – at least in comparison to the puritanical times that followed – as one long outdoor party.' Later, she argues that the price paid for the 'buoyant individualism' of the Renaissance and the Enlightenment, was greater loneliness, disengagement, and a loss of vitality and pleasure in the 'givenness of the world'. Both an inadvertent and deliberate suppression of collective celebration and joy followed. Religions rose which were suspicious of both public displays of uncontrolled enjoyment and the possibility that individuals, working through states of provoked ecstasy, might circumvent the church and establish a direct relationship with God, rendering them redundant. Then there emerged an odd, corrosive compatibility between faiths like Calvinism, and the consequences of a market system excessively focused on the role of the atomized individual. Both induce 'psychic isolation' and 'inner loneliness'. As complex as this historical analysis might appear, the message seems to be quite simple. We must stop working so much, to earn and consume, and start to party. This sounds like heresy. Can less really be more?

Consuming passions

The fundamental flaw in the system has been understood, in fact, from the beginning of the modern economy, and right across the political spectrum. In the eighteenth and nineteenth centuries economic thinkers as diverse as Adam Smith and Karl Marx made the point. Smith, key reference point for globalizing free-marketeers, mocked lovers of luxury who 'walk about loaded with a multitude of baubles . . . some of which may sometimes be of some little use, but all of which might at all times be very well spared, and of which the whole utility is certainly not worth the fatigue of bearing the burden.'

Just under a century later, Marx laid bare the very human dissatisfaction that seemed to drive the spiral of demand for baubles and palaces, suggesting that, 'A house may be large or small; as long as the neighbouring houses are equally small, it satisfies all social requirement for a dwelling. But let a palace arise beside the little house, and it shrinks the house to a hut.'[18]

At the end of the nineteenth century Thorstein Veblen coined the term 'conspicuous consumption' to describe how the burgeoning elite reassured themselves that they stood apart from the masses. They bought more and better of anything that took their fancy – clothes, houses, holidays – in order to stand out from the crowd.

Now, most people in the developed world can fill their pockets with baubles or strive for a house that thinks it's a palace. Why do we appear never to be satisfied? Say our pay goes up, we buy new clothes or move to a new larger house. For a brief while, typically, we will get a buzz of raised satisfaction. But it soon wears off and we quickly return to the 'background' level of satisfaction that we had before our stroke of good fortune, or shopping spree. For most of the things that we see and know intuitively, academics feel compelled to introduce an exotic new terminology, and this is no exception. The fact that the shine quickly wears off the latest purchase is called 'hedonic adaptation'. The fact that we then feel compelled, as a triumph of hope over experience, to buy more, thinking that the next elusive, perfect purchase will finally deliver us into a state of lasting bliss – this is known as being on the 'hedonic treadmill'.

The way in which we acclimatize to new circumstances can have startling outcomes. Barry Schwartz quotes a classic example in his book *The Paradox of Choice*. A range of people who had experienced vastly different fortunes were questioned about levels of happiness. Some had won up to $1 million on the lottery; others had suffered terrible accidents leaving them paraplegic or quadriplegic. Surprisingly, both groups counted themselves to be happy. And while the lottery winners considered themselves happier than did the accident victims, the lottery winners reported levels of happiness that were no different from the general population. Schwartz explains that 'first, people just get used to good or bad fortune. Second, the new standard of what's a good experience (winning the lottery) may make many of the ordinary pleasures of daily life (the smell of freshly brewed coffee, the new blooms and refreshing breezes of a lovely spring day) rather tame by comparison.'[19] And, when surveyed, the lottery winners did indeed report lower levels of satisfaction from life's offering of modest daily pleasures.

The second worm in the apple of consumerism is the way that people unconsciously respond, having adapted to their new circumstances. Both economists and psychologists argue that people are driven to experience pleasure, and that pleasure derives from the novelty of new experiences, before the lustre is lost through familiarity. Once pleasure becomes merely 'comfort', it no longer satisfies, so most people seek out the 'upgrade', to feel once again, if only briefly, the pleasure from novelty. This process of always wanting the larger house, the upgraded digital entertainment hub, or the latest car is what increasingly large numbers of economists accept is part of life on the deeply unsatisfying hedonic treadmill. And the vast majority of us are stuck on it, running like hell and getting nowhere in terms of lasting life satisfaction.

The problem gets even more acute the richer a society gets. Our spending power, the range of products and the pace of innovation all fall into ever accelerating step. Soon after the product is out of the box we are dissatisfied, and start to cast around for new consumption targets. We will generally tire of our gadgets before their built-in obsolescence sends them the same way as their packaging: to landfill. It's a lose-lose situation. Our ecological footprint has gone up, and we are left with a chronic sense of dissatisfaction. An extraordinary study of people's shopping habits busts an enduring myth about the importance of unlimited consumer choice.[20] In separate cases shoppers were offered samples to taste from displays of either six or twenty-four varieties of jam. The bigger range attracted more people but, on average, at both displays individuals tasted about the same number of samples. At the checkout, however, a real difference emerged. People offered the smaller range were ten times more likely to actually make a purchase. The others had been paralysed by too much choice. There are major psychological costs in making choices, and the more you are offered, the higher the cost. So a society that worships consumer choice above more important things (like a habitable planet and caring for those who need it), is a society that is committing itself to high and lasting levels of dissatisfaction (not to mention problems with the planet and wider society). Too much choice really can be a bad thing.

The greatest sacrifice we make to stay on the treadmill is time – for ourselves or to be with friends and family. We pay our debts in work-related stress – the emotional sound track to modern life. We are running in consumer circles, making ourselves feel much worse off. As Schwartz puts it, 'No matter how fast you run on this kind of machine, you still don't get anywhere . . . no matter how good your choices and how pleasurable the results, you still end up back where you started in terms of subjective experience.'[21]

In spite of this, the grip is hard to shake, and for good reason. A huge amount of energy and creativity goes into keeping us hooked on consuming for its own sake. The advertising industry sits like the overseer of old, cracking its whip of consumer discontent to keep everyone in place, turning the well-oiled wheel of the hedonic treadmill. Charles F. Kettering, director of General Motors Research Laboratories, wrote an article in 1929 called 'Keep the Consumer Dissatisfied'. Coming just before the stock market crash of 1929, writes Michael Perelman, professor of economics at California State University,[22] he argued that the 'key to economic prosperity is the organized creation of dissatisfaction . . . If everyone were satisfied no one would want to buy the new thing.'

Decades of advertising-fuelled consumption have led to disturbing, comic or perhaps logical, conclusions. In the US brand identification is so strong that parents are prone to name their children after branded goods: leading in the year 2000 to 353 baby Lexuses, 298 Armanis and 269 Chanels.[23] To many economists, these perversities, delusions and negative impacts on individual well-being are necessary evils. You can't bake a cake of increasing wealth and growing economies without breaking some eggs: social, emotional and ecological costs are part of the deal of contemporary living, they suggest.

But they are looking through the wrong end of the telescope. It isn't simply that consumer culture hasn't delivered us into happiness, or has failed to pay its ecological bills. It has brought with it demonstrable human costs. The rate of serious clinical depression in the US has more than tripled over two generations, and increased tenfold over the twentieth century.[24] Since 1960 in the US the divorce rate doubled; the teenage suicide rate tripled; recorded violent crime quadrupled; and the prison population quintupled.[25]

We're accustomed to thinking that as countries get richer, they also get cleaner and more efficient. But, in some very important ways, the opposite is the case and we have merely exported our ecological impact. This is an issue which, when coupled with the global challenge of poverty reduction, gives us both our biggest problem and greatest opportunity.

Choosing a different life – for everyone

The coincidence of global environmental change and economic globalization forces us to reframe politics in the present and to look again at our future horizon.

An expanding library of research is confirming the folk wisdom that, beyond a certain point, having more stuff doesn't make us happier. This is a revolutionary insight for a consumer society. Liberating the relatively rich from a treadmill of exhausting working weeks will also serve greatly to reduce the burden we place on our environment. None of this, however, relieves the far more urgent burden felt by the hundreds of millions globally who endure real poverty. Indeed it could smack of 'pulling the ladder up behind us'.

For these people, the prospect of longer lives with greater degrees of satisfaction remains a mirage, unless their basic needs are met. That is only likely to happen by raising their levels of consumption: ensuring reliable food, water and sanitation, housing, energy, health and education. With a world already collectively over-consuming its natural resources that can only be achieved if the rich consume less, and we greatly increase the efficiency in our use of resources. The good news is that surprising benefits may result from the former solution. The bad news is that the potential of the latter is probably far more limited than many people realize.

The way that well-being rises along with income breaks down at the point where a person's income is sufficient to guarantee basic material needs. While this figure is quite low, it's a level of earnings that many millions in the world can only dream about. Millions in the world's poorest countries live on less than $1 a day, and very many more live on less than $3 a day – a level up to which, roughly speaking, there is a very strong relationship between life expectancy and income. Conventionally, raising people's income above $1 a day is deemed to be lifting them out of absolute poverty. But even this level co-exists with appallingly high infant mortality rates and cannot be seen in any meaningful sense as an escape from poverty. Without a fundamental change in the distribution of global economic benefits to the world's poorest people, an unimaginably huge, perverse and ecologically destructive growth in the global economy would be called for. Here is the problem. In the last couple of decades the slice of the global economic cake reaching the poorest has shrunk.

Comparing the 1980s to the 1990s, in the earlier decade it took about $45 worth of global economic growth to generate $1 worth of poverty reduction to people living on under $1 a day. But in the 1990s it took $166 worth to do the same. Perversely, with the system we have, the rich have to get very much richer for the poor to get slightly less poor. But in doing so, the levels of consumption of the rich are driving environmental crises which hit the poorest people first and worst.[26]

On current trends, with these already bad, and worsening patterns, unless the rich consume less and the poor capture and keep more of the economic benefits that currently leak to the wealthy, just to lift everyone in the world up to the level of earning at least $3 per day would take the natural resources from in excess of fifteen planets like Earth.

And, as the world is already over-consuming its natural resource base, how do we turn the global consumer ship around? An insight at the core of this book is that the solution can be found wrapped up within the problem.

Our argument goes in completely the opposite direction to the usual caricature of environmentalism. Greens are categorized as demanding a catalogue of denials, limitations, self-accounting, and community bin-policing. In the UK at least, this has now entered the mainstream of politics. We have newly-minted green politicians in every party who are calling for citizens to change their behaviour (though they have so far lacked the confidence to put into place measures that make that easy).

It's not just that the tone of this kind of thinking doesn't set the world alight. These tendencies to limit and control swim against the tide of some of the strongest and most widespread cultural trends of modern, western societies: experiment, self-exploration, establishing new kinds of connection with other people and places. Greens have a reputation for wanting to turn down the music at the party of contemporary living.

Certainly it is important to shine a bright light on some of its perverse and destructive aspects. But the contributors to this book show that, if we get the next few years right, acting on climate change, biodiversity loss and poverty will not just 'save the planet and many of its people', it will also create opportunities to live much better lives.

There is plenty of evidence to show that the rich could lower their levels of consumerism, freeing up 'environmental space' for the poor in which to develop, without the rich undermining their own subjective well-being in any meaningful way. Most people in wealthy countries are already far beyond the point where there is any relationship between their earnings and their life satisfaction. One cause for confidence is that already in Britain there are people living with both very large and relatively small ecological footprints, and each is as likely to be happy as the other. Whether, as this particular survey showed, you enjoy one-planet living, or are consuming at the rate of seven planets, your life satisfaction level will be unaffected. This really does suggest that good lives don't have to cost the Earth.

Managing the transition won't be easy. Psychological research tells us that we easily adapt to lower levels of consuming and end up just as happy as before, but in the short term we can react negatively to the prospect. It's hard to get over the fact that the idea of change is worse than the reality. This is what makes meaningful change so difficult for politicians to contemplate. Of course, as the potential environmental consequences of our current course become more obvious, the balance shifts in that political calculation. But, will it do so fast, or far enough? Let's see what our wide range of contributors think.

Andrew Simms and Joe Smith

Notes to Introduction

1. Sam Thompson, Saamah Abdallah, Nic Marks, Andrew Simms and Victoria Johnson, *The European (un)Happy Planet Index*, nef (the new economics foundation), London, 2007.
2. Calculation by nef based on standard emission figures. The precise time is 08:12 hours, 3 January.
3. *Africa – Up in Smoke? The Second Report of the Working Group on Climate Change and Development*, nef & IIED (International Institute for Environment and Development), London, 2005.
4. *Sub-Saharan Africa: Global Monitoring Report 2007: Confronting the Challenges of Gender Equality and Fragile States*, World Bank, Washington DC.
5. Erik Stokstad, 'Global Loss of Biodiversity Harming Ocean Bounty', *Science*, Vol. 314, no. 5800, 3 November 2006.
6. UK Trade Statistics, http: //www.uktradeinfo.com, HM Revenue and Customs.
7. United Nations Commodity Trade Statistics Database, Statistics Division, http: //comtrade.un.org.
8. 'Briefing: The Use of Palm Oil for Biofuel and as Biomass for Energy', Friends of the Earth, 2006 and Eric Wakker, 'Greasy Palms: The Social and Ecological Impacts of Large Scale Oil Palm Plantation Development in Southeast Asia', Friends of the Earth, 2004.
9. *Peat – CO_2: Assessment of CO_2 Emissions from Drained Peatlands in SE Asia*, Wetlands International, Delft Hydraulics, Alterra Research Center (Wageningen University), Delft, Netherlands, 2006.
10. United Nations Commodity Trade Statistics Database, Statistics Division, http://comtrade.un.org.
11. Andrew Rudin, 'How Improved Efficiency Harms the Environment', 1999, http://home.earthlink.net/~andrew rudin/article.html

12. *The European (un)Happy Planet Index*, 2007.
13. Daniel Gilbert, *Stumbling on Happiness*, Harper Perennial, London, 2006.
14. Alain de Botton, *How Proust can Change your Life*, Picador, London, 1997.
15. Richard Layard, *Happiness: Lessons from a New Science*, Penguin, London, 2005.
16. *The (un)Happy Planet Index*, nef, London, 2006; *The European (un)Happy Planet Index*, 2007.
17. Barbara Ehrenreich, *Dancing in the Streets: A History of Collective Joy*, Granta, London, 2007.
18. Karl Marx (1849: 163), quoted in Michael Perelman, *Manufacturing Discontent: The Trap of Individualism in Corporate Society*, Pluto Press, London, 2005.
19. Barry Schwartz, *The Paradox of Choice: Why More is Less*, HarperCollins, New York, 2004.
20. Quoted in Schwartz, 2004.
21. Ibid.
22. Michael Perelman, *Manufacturing Discontent: The Trap of Individualism in Corporate Society*, Pluto Press, London, 2005.
23. Ibid.
24. Robert E. Lane, *The Loss of Happiness in Market Democracies*, Yale, New Haven and London, 2000.
25. David Myers, a psychologist, writes in *The American Paradox: Spiritual Hunger in an Age of Plenty*, Yale, New Haven and London, 2000.
26. David Woodward and Andrew Simms, *Growth isn't Working: The Unbalanced Distribution of Costs and Benefits from Economic Growth*, nef (the new economics foundation), London, 2006.

1

Having a Good Time

We know something needs to change. But 'buying a ukulele and putting a piano in the kitchen' isn't the most obvious act of planetary redemption. Unless, that is, you are **Tom Hodgkinson**, editor of *The Idler*. Yet even for Tom such a move counts as relatively extreme. Because his main advice for us is that to tackle climate change, possibly the best thing we could do is nothing at all. But he means it literally, not in the sense of just keep on doing what you're doing. He wants us all just to stop and take it easy. No more shopping, no more upgrading consumer durables. The answer, he says, is to 'decommodify our fun'. And, for a little extra guidance, it's hard to argue with his recommendation that, 'the less time one spends in the lonely aisles of Tesco's, the more pleasure comes into your life'.

In case all that pushes you beyond your consumer comfort zone, **David Boyle**, the author of many books, including *Authenticity* and *The Tyranny of Numbers*, reminds us that we've been here before. History tells us that different lives are possible. Without suggesting that we go back in time, he merely points out a few historical ironies. Today, we take progress for granted. But David writes that as long ago as the twelfth century – a time of courtly love, troubadours, and startlingly impressive gothic cathedrals – men were as tall, and women taller than they are today and therefore as well, if not better, fed. He says that in the fifteenth century, the average English peasant 'needed to work for only fifteen weeks to earn the money they needed to survive for the year'.

While, today, we struggle to survive on two full-time salaries. So, perhaps, a little rethink is in order.

David Goldblatt, author of *The Ball is Round: A Global History of Football*, thinks that we all need to play more. But he's not a normal, male sports fanatic. He thinks we've got modern sport all wrong. It's too 'po-faced' and serious. And, like the earnest defence of the 2012 London Olympics, 'couched in terms of renewing infrastructure, tackling social exclusion, and responding to obesity'. Rubbish, says David, in the end, 'it's just a bunch of games – a form of organized, complex play'. And we need more of it. Welcome to more low-carbon fun: sailing, diving, rowing, swimming (all excellent skills for a world of rising sea levels), and walking, running, riding and cycling. Goodbye to: fuel-hungry Formula 1 motor racing, 'the sport of lemmings', and also, probably, golf, a land and water-hungry extension of oppressive, corporate 'workaholism, perfectionism and networking disguised as socializing'.

Tom Hodgkinson

The Art of Doing Nothing

It's the argument of this essay that good lives are cheap, cheerful and will save the planet to boot. It's a win-win-win-win situation.

Recently I interviewed the great American journalist Barbara Ehrenreich. We were talking about her new book, *Dancing in the Streets*, where she argues that the removal of festivity and ritual and regular partying from western culture over the last two or three hundred years is to blame for our current malaise, our ennui, our bipolar disorders, our anxiety, our melancholy. We agreed that the individualist-expansionist-Protestant-capitalist experiment had gone wrong, having caused gloom, despondency and servitude for individuals, and potential environmental disaster for the planet. Clearly, she said, we're going to have to stop doing certain things, like cut down on travel and cars and plastics and oil consumption. 'But you can't have a programme based on giving things up,' she said. That would be too ascetic and self-denying. 'We have to show the world that there is a new world of pleasure and fun out there for the taking.'

Pleasure and fun. These are the keys. We have to carve out an ethical approach that demonstrates that good lives, far from costing the Earth, will actually save the Earth. We need to show that the good life does mean giving things up, it means grabbing hold of a new life, one far richer and more enjoyable than the money-and-status dream that motivates us today.

What is the good life? What would a good life consist of? For me the essential components would be enjoyable work, lots of sitting around doing nothing, lots of parties and dancing and beer and wine. So that's good meaning 'pleasurable' and 'satisfying'. The other meaning of good, of course, is the moral one: good as the opposite to evil. This I would define as 'tending to improve the common interest'. Good lives are not about erecting a wall around ourselves and shutting out everyone else. Good lives should be about constantly improving the lives of other people. This is what was meant by the old medieval ideas of salvation through good works: if you poured love and care into your every action, then you were going straight to heaven. I don't mean that this should be done in a 'look at me, I'm such a caring person' way. There's nothing worse than organized, institutionalized charities which guarantee the donor a nice warm compassionate feeling. What I mean is a genuinely generous attitude, where we give without thought of what will be given back. This way lies freedom.

It's true that at first sight, the good life – for which also read the idle life, the free life, the green life – looks rather negative. No holidays, no cars, no taxis, no restaurants, no supermarkets, no orange squash, no breakfast cereals. But in actual fact it is enormously liberating and, yes, fun. This thought struck my partner and I three or four years ago when we going through a financial crisis. Heads in hands at the kitchen table, backs of envelopes and the calculator before us, we scratched our heads and planned economies. No more newspapers or magazines. Grow some vegetables. Write down everything you spend.

At first this belt-tightening exercise might have seemed miserable. But gradually we discovered that a new world was opening up for us. Taking hold of the reins allowed us greater freedom. And what was the problem anyway? We ate well, we drank well, we had friends to stay. And we'd decided that there were two areas where we would not cut down, and they were childcare and alcohol. Getting a girl in to play with the children so that we could sleep or work or clean seemed sensible. And life in the nuclear family without beer and wine seemed a dismal prospect.

Gradually we found that thrift, far from being a self-denying virtue, was a positive and joyful one. As G.K. Chesterton wrote in his essay 'The Romance of Thrift', 'thrift is creative'. It is creative because it is anti-waste. When you make four meals out of one chicken, you are being creative. When you throw it away after one meal, you are being wasteful. Thrift is also anti-capitalist. Capitalism loves waste. Waste is at its essence. Waste means money. It means more spending.

But a good life means plenty and abundance as opposed to a sickening glut, which is the capitalist way. The old-fashioned method of living was to eat frugally and then enjoy an enormous blow-out every two or three weeks. These blow-outs were built into the religious calendar and were called feast days. The frugality itself tended to intensify the pleasure of the feast. I gave up booze for Lent this year. My motivation was partly centred around the anticipation of the pleasure of getting back on to it again. It was for this reason that the Puritans hated Lent and the very idea of fasting: it was actually a pleasure-based idea, not a self-denying one.

But anyway, it's important to recognize that the opposite to the excesses of consumer capitalism is not some sort of boring Cromwellian, Leninist world where there are no maypoles and no rich purple velvets (as well as banning dancing and music, Cromwell banned colour: natural fibres only). I have found in my own life that the less time one spends in the lonely aisles of Tesco's, the more pleasure comes into your life.

Nor am I looking at some sort of arid Tony Benn utopia where all the proles are fully employed in the factories and cheerfully cycle to their union-protected paradise with a cheery grin on their faces and corned beef sandwiches in their baskets.

No. We are going to smash that system, not through socialism, which is the imposition of order by a do-gooding little humourless oligarchy; not through capitalism, which subjugates human beings in order to make giant profits for the oligarchy, but through personal anarchy and a radical reinvention of what really matters. Right now we have a moralizing Government and a sick and bloated private sector, which steals from the poor and gives to the rich (it's called Tesco's). Tesco's is merely banditry dressed up as a supermarket.

So how do we smash the system? Well, very simply, we do nothing. Or at least, we do a lot less. Doing is the problem. The green movement suffers from the same delusions as its supposed enemy. This is the idea that 'something must be done'. When we worry and fret about global warming, when we fly around the world to attend conferences and discuss what must be done (which often boils down to the ludicrous suggestion 'write to your MP'), we add to the problem. Recently in *The Idler* we ran an article with the title 'How To Save The Planet Without Really Trying'. The argument put forward, by the author Stephan Harding of Dartington College, was that it is precisely man's scurrying around, his self-important interference, this urge to 'do' things, that has caused all the problems in the first place. If we had had the good sense simply to sit around and contemplate the heavens rather than plundering and subjecting the entire world and its people, then we wouldn't have got into this fine mess in the first place. Truly, we are nothing more than blundering Laurel and Hardys, and anyone who thinks different is a self-deluded loon. Nothing matters! Well, Harding argued that the best way to prevent global catastrophe is to refrain from 'doing'. Instead of marching, picketing, writing letters and all the rest of the ineffective panoply of consumer action, just go and lie on a hillside. Get out of the way. Don't go on holiday. Don't drive a car. Don't bother.

If you read *The Economist*, you will learn that capitalism, or 'business' as they call it, after being initially hostile to the green movement, has now embraced it wholeheartedly. This is because they have realized that there are massive new profits in store. And why? Because of new technology. New technology means money. Upgrading means money. Throwing away the old and bringing in the new means money. It means more growth and that's what they love: growth. They love growth because the whole system depends on greed: I buy shares in a certain company because I want those shares to increase in value faster than inflation. Therefore it is not actually the bottom line that interests business, it is rate of growth. But they can only grow by feeding, and feeding very greedily: feeding on human labour, or by mining the Earth for its resources. No one is interested in companies that stay the same size: 0 per cent growth means death to business.

So be wary of the green movement. To me it looks very much like the other side of the same coin, in that it involves a lot of hard work and a lot of money-spending. The good life avoids both. We need also to be on our guard against the Puritan-socialist strain in the green movement, which looks to me a lot like Methodism in the way it imposes austerity on other people, and can come across very much as anti-pleasure. And too much worrying! Worrying is itself a capitalist concept, like the future. Worrying leads to the purchase of more stuff as we try to shore up our anxieties with objects.

I think we need to philosophize. That is the first step. Don't do something; just sit there. We need to think and reflect and pause. We need to stare out of the window and get a distance on the whole thing. We need to abandon fear and the first fear we need to abandon is the fear of not having enough money.

Of course we need to be sensible about money. We need to earn it to pay rent and buy food. But do we need it for fun? I would argue that we need to separate fun from money. Today the illusion governs us that when we are released from our boring jobs, we should then pour our wages into various fun machines, such as TVs, cinema, fancy restaurants, package holidays, cruises, holidays, trips to South Molton Street or the local mall, football matches, amusement arcades. Make your own fun! Nail together two bits of wood – hey presto, a sword!

There is another great advantage to not spending money, and that is that it is so cheap. When you reduce your outgoings, you reduce your dependence on wages. When you reduce your dependence on wages, you do not need to work so hard. So thrift leads directly to idleness and self-sufficiency. Idleness creates time during which you can do things which save money.

We need to decommodify our fun. Take the example of festivals. Clearly, festivals like Glastonbury are popular because they fulfil a human need for festivity and ritual. For three days, our normal world is turned upside-down. But they are so costly. A proper festival should be free, like Notting Hill Carnival, where we really do dance in the streets. Round where I live in Devon, I have been lucky enough to get involved in a local music festival. For three days, our village is filled with bands and DJs and roving minstrels. The wonderful thing about it is that it's free. There is no enclosure, no inside or outside, no security guards, no wristbands: bands play by the seaside on the main stage and then all over town in the pubs and cafes. The whole thing is organized and run by unpaid volunteers. The removal of any profit incentive keeps the thing high quality and harmonious: we may disagree sometimes but our aim is shared. The cost of the festival is raised through auctions, grants, sponsorship, donations, merchandise, running a bar and renting stall space to traders.

Local businesses love it because the streets are filled with punters all weekend. It's a brilliant system and we'd be happy to give hints and tips to anyone who would like to start something similar in their area.

My other suggestions include buying a ukulele and putting a piano in the kitchen. These are not intended as rules to follow but more an indicator of a certain sort of approach to life: we mend and we make our own fun. We bake bread and we put tomatoes on the windowsill. Each loaf baked and each broad bean podded from our own garden is one in the face for the Tescos of this world. And baking bread is a great pleasure, as well as being a hell of a lot cheaper and a hell of a lot better than the factory-made teeth-clogging stuff you get in the shops.

The alternative to capitalism is not the self-denial of a monk. It is not a serious-minded, Puritan austerity. It is rather the embracing of a new world of pleasure and fun and freedom. When you stop working and stop spending you start living.

David Boyle

We Have Been Here Before

> 'I have been here before,' I said; I had been there before;
> first with Sebastian more than twenty years ago on a cloud-
> less day in June, when the ditches were white with fool's-
> parsley and meadowsweet and the air heavy with all the
> scents of summer.
>
> Evelyn Waugh, Brideshead Revisited

I am a member of the generation that was brought up, probably more than any other, with the myth of progress. As we grew
up, all around us the urban motorways and the tower blocks
were driving out the high streets, parks and terraced avenues.

They still are today, of course, but then the ideological
purpose was stronger. It was done in the name of 'progress',
which we were constantly told it was impossible to obstruct.

We know a little better now. We can see that the kind of
'progress' peddled by the establishment at that time meant
little more than change: and many of those changes did not
amount to real progress at all. We could have stood in the way
of them after all, and we might all have been better off if we
had. Certainly the planet would have been.

In the decades since, most professional disciplines have
dispensed with the idea of inevitable progress. Second-hand
bookshops are littered with titles of forgotten historians
peddling the idea, though it clings manfully to the discipline
of economics, which assumes that more money inevitably
means progress. If the economy grows, economics assumes
that it has progressed: change is progress.

This is nonsense of course. But it means that, built into the basic DNA of economics is an assumption that now is better than then, and so influential have economists been over the past century that we have come to share their assumptions. We dismiss the medieval centuries as dark periods of brutality, lawlessness and poverty. We shrink from their concepts of dentistry and thank goodness – probably correctly – that we live now.

But those who began to criticize industrial capitalism for the way it generated poverty, social collapse and environmental crisis, were also influenced by aspects of medieval economics which we now forget. People like Ruskin, Morris or Hilaire Belloc particularly looked to the Middle Ages for their inspiration, and especially the twelfth century, the era of courtly love, troubadours and gothic cathedrals. In fact, there is now some evidence for giving the twelfth century a second look.

When archaeologists unearth skeletons in London from that period, they are as tall, and therefore as well fed, as skeletons in any other period of history except our own. In the case of women, they are even slightly taller. They lived in a society that built some of the greatest works of art humanity is capable of: in three centuries, the limestone quarries of northern Europe produced more stone for gothic cathedrals than was used in all ancient Egypt to build the pyramids. Certainly there was famine and poverty, but that was brought about by war. For the most part, the hundreds of thousands of small independent farmers produced unprecedented and debt-free economic security – with more days off for the average farm worker than anything people now enjoy.

We may not want to catapult ourselves back there, but it is still worth wondering why – despite two centuries of economic growth – we seem unable to afford lives or cathedrals anything like theirs. Victorian economists calculated that the average English peasant in 1485 needed to work fifteen weeks a year to earn the money they needed to survive for the year. In 1564, it was forty weeks. Now, of course, it is questionable whether we can manage to afford a reasonable life in Britain without two salaries all the year round.

In the same way that we have become used to the idea of grinding poverty in the Middle Ages, we have also become used to the idea that it was a period of vicious laissez-faire, where any new entrepreneur could carve a swathe through any community or environmental obstacle. It is true that the medieval period was one of massive expansion in trade. In fact, global trade took until the eighteenth century to recover to the level it was before the Black Death. But medieval economists were very aware of the limits to growth and the need to regulate their over-use.

The first Royal Commission on air pollution was set up by Edward I in 1285, and anyone who wanted to do any business – or make any feudal payment – was regulated by a mixture of rules, customs and reciprocal understandings designed to reduce conflict and defend the fish stocks. A hen had to be accepted as payment, must be accepted even if it looked sickly, if it could be scared into jumping the garden fence. Millers were not allowed to let the river water rise so high behind their dam to prevent a bee standing on top and drinking without wetting its wings.

They sound quaint today, when we have the instruments to measure reciprocity exactly, but they worked. If there were medieval concepts of the market or consumer society – and there were constant complaints about luxuries bought and debt incurred (charging interest was forbidden by the church) – they were subservient to ordinary morality. If someone forced people to buy at a high price, that was regarded as a form of usury. There was a 'just price' that should be charged, and if it was undercut or overtaken too far, then somebody was considered to be suffering.

It was naïve in a sense. Later medieval monarchs, like Isabella of Castile, spent considerable energy investigating why gold was disappearing from her kingdom, having no knowledge of the basic principles of balance of payments. Issues like inflation were regarded wholly as moral questions, rather than wholly economic ones as – rightly or wrongly – we see them today.

We may not agree with any morality that understood economic processes so little. But something of that underlying medieval approach to economics – underpinned by morality – survives to this day. When Coca-Cola built cold drinks dispensers that raised the price according to the prevailing temperature, there was an outcry. The fair trade and ethical sector in the UK, which began so small a generation ago, now stands at £29 billion a year – that's bigger than alcohol or tobacco sales. People increasingly want an ethical coherence in their lives. It makes no sense to them, as perhaps it did to their parents, to campaign against companies that despoil the environment or undermine lives, yet to have their pension money invested in Shell, British Nuclear Fuels or Tesco.

The new economy, with morality back at the heart, is more human than the classic economic idea – peddled until recently – that really believed people always maximized the money values of every economic interaction. We all know in our own lives that many other considerations apply. And once we realize that money is a poor way of measuring progress, one that is literally unravelling the life systems of the Earth, we begin to wonder how on earth morality and economics ever got divorced in the first place. How did market economics, invented by moral philosopher Adam Smith, make the break? How did we end up with the cult of the CEO *übermensch*, for whom ordinary morality does not apply?

But in the intervening period since Smith, many of the fiercest critics of amoral economics, back to William Cobbett,

John Ruskin and William Morris, have looked to the medieval period as inspiration. It is, in fact, the heart of a great lost political tradition of agrarian radicalism. Those who espoused it have been dismissed as unconnected cranks, throwbacks to a medieval arcadia which never existed. They have been treated as romantic artists whose trespass into the political arena was an unfortunate blot on the lives of otherwise exemplary men of letters. But seen in their true light, they are actually different expressions of the same tradition. And more than that. They are the tip of the iceberg, while below the surface the great tradition is stirring again.

They seem to have slotted indiscriminately into every other possible political tradition: Radicals (Cobbett), Tories (Ruskin, or so he said), Socialists (Morris), Liberals (Chesterton and Belloc), Greens (Schumacher), even out and out Blackshirts (Henry Williamson). Yet what holds them together is remarkably consistent: bitter scepticism about the conventional values of wealth, power and money, and the delusion of money as a measure of value compared to the values of nature – and more than that: a spiritual sense of what good, creative human life might be.

Out of this tradition, eight decades ago, emerged a coherent critique of conventional economics that formed itself into a political campaign to shift the debate against giant corporations and big government. They became known as the Distributists, and they were inspired by Hilaire Belloc's 1912 book *The Servile State*, an influential diatribe against big business and Fabian collectivist policies, now rather inappropriately kept in print by obscure American libertarians, which wouldn't have pleased him.

Distributism knitted together the old Catholic social doctrine of Pope Leo XIII that was so close to Belloc's heart, inspired originally by Ruskin via Cardinal Manning. It mixed a generous dollop of land reforming Liberalism with unworldly Gandhian simplicity, borrowing the old slogan of Joseph Chamberlain and Jesse Collings from the 1880s, 'three acres and a cow'. At its heart was the redistribution of land and property so that everyone had some – on the ground that small enterprises, smallholdings and small units were the only basis for dignity, independence and liberty.

Belloc and his friend G.K. Chesterton and the Distributists were equally hostile to socialism and capitalism, and set out to prove they were the same thing, and that both tended towards slavery. They were anti-industrial, anti-finance, anti-corporation, anti-bureaucrat, and most of all anti-giantism, either big bureaucracy or big business – the 'Big Rot' according to Belloc. What it was actually for was a little hazier, but it included Jeffersonian solutions of workers' co-operatives, smallholdings and land redistribution, and savings boosted by the state. Capitalism is unable to satisfy human needs for stability, sufficiency and security, said Belloc, and is therefore only a phase.

One of their earliest campaigns was in support of the small London bus companies that were being driven out by the monopolistic London General Omnibus Company. In response, they bought a series of Distributist buses, painted them red, green and blue and called them names like 'William Morris' – and took on the big company buses. It didn't work.

But while Belloc provided the ideological underpinning, Chesterton provided the rhetorical firepower. His passionate denunciation of corporate power, of 'clone town' corporate shopping – not shops at all, he said, but 'branches of the accountancy profession' – was based on a sense that neither corporate power nor consumerism could provide for people's material or spiritual needs, and that both implied a mechanical tyranny that was increasingly wielded over people as the monopolies took hold.

He claimed he had only twice been censored by newspaper editors and once it had been for criticizing big shops – one of those things you were no longer allowed to say. 'I think the big shop is a bad shop', he wrote in *An Outline of Sanity*, 'I think it bad not only in a moral but a mercantile sense; that is, I think shopping there is not only a bad action but a bad bargain. I think the monster emporium is not only vulgar and insolent, but incompetent and uncomfortable; and I deny that its large organization is efficient.'

Chesterton and Belloc thundered from their respective platforms, or in the pages of Chesterton's newspaper *G.K.'s Weekly*, or debated with Fabians like Shaw and Wells. But the real vulnerability about Distributism was that it lacked practical policy solutions. 'I think we can explain how to make a small shop or a small farm a common feature of our society better than Matthew Arnold explained how to make the State the organ of Our Best Self', wrote Chesterton, but he in fact couldn't. The whole prospect seemed impossible, and the very tone of both men was melancholic, as if the tidal wave of giantism would inevitably sweep them away: 'Do anything, however small', urged Chesterton in 1926. 'Save one out of a hundred shops. Save one croft out of a hundred crofts. Keep one door open out of a hundred doors; for so long as one door is open, we are not in prison.'

Distributism fizzled out after the Second World War. Their land schemes of the 1940s failed and the Distributist League was wound up in the 1950s. There have been Distributist gestures from governments since then (Mrs Thatcher's sale of council houses, for example), but little more. Its proponents were disappointed that those who had taken it to heart most were not the urban poor, but craftsmen like Eric Gill or journalists like Beachcomber. Once Chesterton had joined Belloc in the Roman Catholic Church, then Distributists were increasingly regarded as the political wing of Catholicism. Today they are all but forgotten, and those who worry about such things are liable to remind anyone mentioning them that

Belloc was an admirer of Franco's and that Chesterton's vitriol for the financial services industry looked worryingly like anti-Semitism.

These are important criticisms, and there is a long history of radical movements in this tradition shifting dangerously to the right once they are worn out (the American Populist Party became white supremacists). But in the defence of Belloc and Chesterton, both men were among the first to recognize Hitler for what he was and to condemn his anti-Semitic policies from the outset.

The point is that, a mere eighty years ago, there was a pioneering group of campaigners who saw what we now see – that giant corporations and giant agencies tend to transform their clients and customers into semi-slaves, prefer their behaviour to be standardized and reward and punish them accordingly. That capitalism and socialism both tend likewise towards tyranny. That the muddle between money and well-being is not just an awkward error but is a threat to human life. Who saw also that the divorce between economics and ethics, and between human beings and the land, is both disabling and corrupting, and dangerous.

We may not recognize their solution of a return to agriculture, and the distribution of small-scale property and land. We may not admire their language about the promotion of a new peasantry. But we can see where they came from.

What we have now, which they could not see, is the glimmers of a revival of sanity. The revival of allotments are testament to people's frustration with supermarket standardization, and the demand for fresh, local food. For the first time since the war, seed companies report selling more vegetable seeds than flower seeds. People campaign against supermarkets, and ethical investment now edges towards £5 billion in the UK alone.

In short, something is in the air. We no longer quite accept the mechanical and reductionist trappings of consumerism.

We are some way from a revolt against it, but the first winds of the storm are blowing.

We also have some practical tools which the Distributists lacked. We can analyse local money flows, to prove that supermarket expansion, cheap flights and motorway construction are precisely the reverse of what is claimed for them: they are, in fact, impoverishing. We have concepts like local currencies, green taxation and fair trade, and they are popular and increasingly so.

Belloc's 'Ha'nacker Mill', one of his most famous poems, is a vision of England in ruins, a microcosm of agrarian and moral collapse. It ends:

> Ha'nacker's down and England's done.
> Wind and Thistle for pipe and dancers,
> *And never a ploughman under the sun:*
> *Never a ploughman. Never a one.*

But there is no longer any need to be quite so despairing. The forces conspiring to prevent us living good lives that don't cost the Earth are hugely powerful. The peril that humanity faces, and the planet we live on, is urgent and dire. The concept of progress remains stolen from us and is wielded by the other side. But we are now waking up, and there is a long and honourable tradition before our time which we can draw on – even learn from. We don't have to work out everything afresh, and we are not alone.

David Goldblatt

How Do you Play?

Uruguayan writer Eduardo Galleano argues, 'Show me how you play and I will show who you are.' The games we play and don't play, how we play them and with whom, have become a central component of the modern world's popular cultures and their understanding of themselves.

'The very symbol, the outward and visible expression of the drive and push and rush and struggle of the raging, tearing, booming nineteenth century!' Mark Twain spoke these words at Delmonico's, a New York restaurant, in April 1889. He was talking about baseball and celebrating the return home of Alfred Spalding's infamous global baseball tour – an exercise in sports goods branding and global cultural imperialism before Michael Jordan was even a twinkle in Phil Knight's eye. Spalding, the Chicago White Sox and the American All-Stars had crossed continents and oceans to play hundreds of games in countries from Australia to Egypt to England. They convinced almost nobody of the virtues of the game but on a wave of expansionist euphoria and boosterism they sealed baseball's place as the central metaphor and pleasure of American sporting culture and urban history.

What then will be the symbol, the outward and visible expression of the cautious, uncertain, harried, complex, twenty-first century? What sports and what sporting cultures might rise to the challenge of reflecting the globally sustainable society that is the precondition of any of us living any kind of good life over the next one hundred years?

This is not a topic that environmentalists and social activists have engaged with in any great detail. Indeed, there continue to be various shades of progressive opinion that are at best uncomfortable with sport as both a participative culture and a professional spectacle. It appears at the margins of debates about urban space, education and public health. But this policy talk is all remarkably po-faced, couched in terms of renewing infrastructure, tackling social exclusion and responding to obesity. All of which is perfectly legitimate but misses the central point about sport – that it is, in the end, just a bunch of games – a form of organized, complex play.

The realm of play, as even the most casual engagement with children reveals, is one of delight, experimentation and creativity. It is a form of social interaction that insists upon collective rule-making and changing, turn-taking and reciprocity, imagination, ebullience, laughter and amazement. If finding ways to defend and even expand the social space in which this can occur is not a serious task I don't know what is. If these are not necessary conditions of the good life I don't want to play.

Environmentalists have not been alone in overlooking this. Indeed, one of the strongest arguments against thinking about sport politically and trying to incorporate it into a vision of the good life is the dismal record of the ideologies that have sought to do so hitherto. Consider Muscular Christianity in the service of imperialism, varieties of Social Darwinism and ultra-nationalism hell bent on hardening the nation for war, and the ludicrous bread and circuses of fascism, Latin American populist authoritarianism and European communists. The hollow, haughty and hypocritical internationalism of the mainstream Olympic movement hardly offers an attractive model.

That's a lot of sport and a lot expected of it without any recognition of the very thing that we relish most about it – its playfulness. However, abandoning the politics of sport or pretending sport does not have a political dimension isn't going to be an effective response. Similarly, sport is rightly criticized for historic and contemporary forms of racism, sexism, homophobia, and discriminatory attitudes towards the disabled. However, that goes for pretty much all cultural practice and institutions. So what are we going to do, pretend it isn't happening and hope it goes away?

Sport is equally despised for its relentless instrumental reason – that is, the centrality of winning and losing, the preference for competition over cooperation. This is a logic that inexorably terminates in everything from the pathological over-engagement of parents in junior football to the corruption, match-fixing, cheating and drug-taking in professional sport. Simultaneously, sport is cast as a trivial, a depthless, meaningless and now irredeemably commodified circus; an instrument for disabling rather than merely manipulating consciousness.

However, to see sport as instrumental reason writ large is to indulge its own internal pretensions. The overweening importance of winning is an illusion that we all maintain for the convenience and motivation of professional sports people. Sport is just a form of organized play, and play that is entirely orientated towards outcomes is no longer a game. Most sport, most of the time, is about losing or drawing. Only one team can win the championship each year, the rest must lose. We continue to take our pleasures from defeat, near misses, occasional success and gloomy mediocrity. Moreover, sport is an arena in which people are acutely aware of and sensitive to the presence of alien forms of instrumental reason. The baleful influence of money and power on sporting events and cultures, be it tycoons who try to buy glory or states that try to decree it, is almost universally abhorred.

Viewing sport as a complex form of play, pleasure and performance allows us to see the triviality of sport from a new perspective. Sport's other-worldliness rests not on its meaninglessness but its ludicrousness. Calculated by the stern and quantifiable metrics of utility, efficiency and safety, sports are nonsense. Using metal sticks to whack a tiny ball across half a kilometre of sculpted landscape into a hole that most rabbits would find a challenge is serious? If you wanted to put the ball in the back of the net, why on earth would you manically kick it rather than calmly carry it? Sport demands of its participants and spectators a leap of faith and the suspension of reason.

Shorn of these misconceptions, sport appears as an essential component of a sane and balanced civilization: a zone in which experimentation, creativity and laughter flourish; a form of performance art that offers its particular aesthetic and kinetic pleasures; an object of civic and communal pride. Above all sport as a spectacle with its apparatus of challenges, contests, competitions, unknown outcomes and final definitive results is a vast polymorphous machine for generating improvised and compressed stories.

What kind of stories will we tell, what kinds of sports will generate the narratives that appeal to us and reflect the temper of our times? Our future sporting culture will thankfully not be made by climate change activists, academics and politicians, but by the pleasures, preferences and performances of the global sporting public. Nonetheless, thinking about a sporting culture that reflects and contributes to a sustainable global society is an interesting thought experiment.

First, there will be more rather than less sport. More in the sense that more people will play more sports, more often throughout their lives and will have more fun while playing them. Given that we are all going to be cutting down on our consumption and production, and let us hope our levels of administration, what do you plan to be doing? I plan to be playing, watching, commenting and reflecting. I hope to do so as a small part of a wider, diverse, participative, reflective and carnivalesque culture of sport. As an old Victorian gentleman once said, 'In the morning I play badminton, in the afternoon I'll go to the ball game and after dinner I'll debate the week's football gossip.' This culture does not include, I hasten to add, the neurotic and narcissistic use of the gym as an instrument of body politics rather than sports conditioning.

Although enhanced participation is no guarantee of wisdom or wit, one hopes that our sporting culture, in keeping with more restrained times, will be less celebrity-driven, less commercially distorted and less prone to hysterical hype. It will speak in many and varied tones, not confined to ex-professionals and anodyne summarizers. It will not however be squeaky clean or holier than thou. There will, I hope, continue to be drinking, carousing, gamesmanship of every kind, gambling and bad language when required.

Second, in what will be the most globalized economic and political order in human history, football is and will be the global sport. While some will lament this, we are in fact very lucky to have stumbled upon a game of such supreme openness, universality and flexibility; features which have guaranteed its unequalled geographical and demographic reach. A cosmopolitan world requires its moment of global communion, structured ritual opportunities to look at itself. The World Cup in particular delivers this more effectively and entertainingly than any other comparable cultural event. In addition, football's unpredictability and spontaneity offer the metaphorical materials for a world faced by an unprecedented level of the former and in desperate need of the latter.

However, this is not to argue for the incipient monoculture that threatens British sporting culture, where the hype and the coverage and the money inexorably drain towards the football beneath. Moreover, it behoves football, of all sports, to directly address the fundamental problems of money and power in global sport more openly, directly and speedily than any other – a task that its current governors have been slow to recognize. In short, football's institutions of regional and global governance need to be opened up, democratized, and made accountable to football's many constituencies. Similarly, the influence of private capital and corporate sponsors in the ownership and direction of professional football must be curtailed.

Third, all sport, professional and amateur, producers and consumers, will be bound by the same imperatives that any social and economic actors will face in a low carbon economy. Issues around energy and water use, location of facilities, transport planning and social inclusion will no doubt lead to a very different geography of facilities than hitherto created by suburban car cultures. However, some sports will find the tasks harder than others.

Step forward motor sports. Seriously, guys, yes you in the fast cars, peak oil is here or near. What are your great-grandchildren going to think a hundred years from now when they look back and see you spunking up the last precious drops of gasoline though the chicane. Will they laugh or cry? I know all that man and machine, technology and humanity, need for speed shtick, but it's just not plausible. Motor racing was the sport of the futurists when the future looked rather more promising than it does currently. Today it looks closer to the sport of lemmings.

Alpine sports are in the front line of climate change, as the steadily diminishing pistes testify. Their fate will run, one suspects, directly parallel to that of motor sports. On even the good news projections of a mere 3°C increase in global ambient temperatures, the Alpine luge could be history long before they put Silverstone and Indianapolis into mothballs. I will mourn the passing of ski-jumping in particular: where else will Finnish teenagers take the angst and their ecstasy?

On the other hand, the hanging political economy of energy and transport should, one imagines, provide a considerable cultural and practical fillip to alternatives including walking, running, cycling and riding. Skateboarding and surfing, one hopes, will retain something of their outsider status and their grassroots rejection of structured competition. All of these however may be superseded in practical as well as metaphorical weight if sea levels rise at the most dramatic end of the scale – expect a resurgence in rowing, small boat sailing, swimming and diving.

The fate of golf intrigues me most, for if in the twentieth century football was the game of the collective industrial, urban working classes, then in the twenty-first century golf is the game of the individualized, post-industrial, suburban middle classes. As a game it possesses that same kind of workaholism, perfectionism and networking disguised as socializing that are essential in the economic realm inhabited by its participants and fans. No account of our age is complete without some grasp on this phenomenon. Given its bucolic aesthetics it might be expected to possess a lighter resource footprint and a greater environmental consciousness than most sports, but the relentless and reckless expansion of the game in its current forms suggests not; from water shortages in Spain, to land shortages in Thailand, golf has added unsustainability to its historic patterns of social exclusion.

Whether low carbon golf is possible, I don't know. The world's links courses are in trouble whatever and the tourist courses of Andalucía are surely just a degree or so Celsius away from desertification. In one plausible, if depressing scenario, the game will enter its twilight as the strictest reserve of the über-elite in a water-short, land-ravaged world. Perhaps it will survive in more populist forms in a version of its original played on heathland and moorland, and peripheral landscapes, where golfing poachers will steal a round by night from the gated preserves of the elite? Perhaps one of the cut down technologically-modified urban forms of the game that have been played will flourish as a guerrilla pastime. Let us hope that sport will tell us more than a tragic narrative of our past environmental misdemeanours and our contemporary inequalities. If we choose to create a participative, reflective and playful sporting culture, we might even have a comedy on our hands.

2

Love, Happiness and Telling Tales

This book is about two stories: how did we get ourselves into this environmental mess, and how are we going to get ourselves out? **Philip Pullman** is one of our greatest living storytellers. So, we asked him what he thought of the tales that environmentalists tell? Were they any good? His answer, unsurprisingly, merely raised more questions. They are part of the 'prophetic tradition' of the Old Testament he said, which is a problem, because many of those prophets were 'hounded out of the city and cast adrift on the waves'. But, he also says that the ecologists' tale is a vital one. It tells 'a story about us and our place in the universe . . . Why are we here? What is here, what does it consist of? What have we got to do now we are here? What responsibilities does being conscious place on us?' Having multiplied our questions, Pullman then reminds us that if we get the answers wrong, we should fear the wrath of nature, perhaps manifest in the avenging polar bears from his trilogy, *His Dark Materials*. In a warming world, angered at the loss of their ice and facing extinction, they might just leap from the pages of fiction to devour us.

Philosopher **A.C. Grayling** warns about being seduced by two-dimensional ciphers of the good life. We are caught, he writes, between two deceptions. On one hand we are blinded by the flashbulbs of the paparazzi into wanting the chimerical and often tragic lifestyles of film and television celebrities.

And, at the other extreme, we are hypnotized by the prospect of retreating to a faux rural idyll. We must beware advertising's 'mirror of dreams'. The truth about where to find real good lives lies much closer to home. It is a matter, he argues, of learning to see afresh and act upon age-old insights drained of meaning by their overuse in a thousand clichés. 'Money and possessions do not yield more than temporary happiness,' he writes, 'true wealth lies in such intangibles as health and love.' What is different today? Our new circumstance of acute environmental crises breathes life into this well-trodden wisdom. Impassable ecological obstacles now lie on the path down which we chase the shadows of conspicuous consumption to deliver our well-being. But another way is not only possible, writes Grayling, it is better, richer and more enduring.

Oliver James, the leading psychologist, offers another cautionary tale about how we look for happiness in the wrong places. In this case, he tells the tale of how his father and grandfather were blinded by the great English obsession: property. Like many others, both invested a little too much of their identity in their homes and the vagaries of the property markets, and both paid the price. He says it is part of the virulent Affluenza virus which works by causing the host to place 'too high a value upon money, possessions, appearances and fame'. We must beware, he says, insecurities created in childhood that fuel status-seeking consumerism later in life.

One lazy accusation this book might invite is that only the secure middle classes can afford the luxury of turning their backs on consumerism. If you're poor, runs the argument, of course you'll aspire to the big house, nice car and foreign holidays. And anyone who questions that is cruelly denying someone their innate right to consume. But **John Bird**, founder of *The Big Issue* magazine for the homeless, grew up surrounded by poverty and violence and he rejects the notion. 'I cycle, I hardly drive a car, I live in a small house, and I rarely go on foreign holidays', he says. 'If I have a holiday, more often than not it's in England. I use local transport, I have a small television, I haven't got a plasma, I go to the cinema when I want to go out and when I do, I usually go by bike or bus.' Bird is more concerned with things that he believes undermine quality of life. All around he sees the negative consequences of powerful monopolies, both public and private, that take away our ability to make choices and control our destinies – something that is vital to well-being. It could result from central government not giving enough power to communities, or giant supermarkets with too much power controlling the local economy. Bird insists that 'a good life is a conscious life, one that is lived with awareness'.

Philip Pullman

(in conversation with Andrew Simms)

The Shape of a Life and the Stories we Tell

Q: Environmentalists must engage people if there is to be a mass shift to lifestyles that do not cost the Earth. What can they learn about the art of storytelling, and who influenced you as a storyteller?

Milton was an enormous influence for me. As William Blake said, 'The reason Milton wrote in fetters when he wrote Angels and God, and at liberty when of Devils and Hell, is because he was a true poet and of the Devil's party without knowing it.' You can tell that his imagination, although not his conscious mind perhaps, pretty passionately disliked God, because everything he gives God to say, every action God takes, is whining, carping, moaning, criticizing, boasting. It's a very unattractive figure, the God of Milton. The son, Messiah, is slightly more attractive, and Satan utterly compelling.

Environmentalists also tell a story about us and ourselves and our place in the universe. In a sense it's a religious story, because that's the big question of religion. Why are we here? What is here, what does it consist of? What have we got to do now we are here? What responsibilities does being conscious place on us? And those are questions which the environmental movement, over the past twenty-five years, and certainly since the global warming issue has come up, has been very much engaged in. What does it mean to us to be conscious of what we are doing to the world?

Some people attempt to maintain a state of denial, 'It's not happening', or 'It is happening, but it's natural and it's nothing to do with us.' Or, 'It's happening but we can fix it with technology.' All these are attempts to deny responsibility for it; to deny anything that they might have to do. So, the questions, the stories that the global warming prophets tell us (let's call them that to distinguish them from the sceptics), take their place right slap bang in the middle of the prophetical tradition, along with the prophets of the Old Testament.

But the prophets of the Old Testament were not very successful because they were generally hounded out of the city and cast adrift on the waves. People don't like hearing what prophets tell them: it's generally uncomfortable. It's full of doom; it's full of warnings; it's full of denunciations and threats to mend their ways or suffer for it. So it's not a popular message. And the struggle that the climate change prophets have had to undertake to get their message heard, I suppose, is similar. But I've noticed a real change in the last year.

Q: Is there an allusion to climate change buried in your trilogy His Dark Materials?

The thing that really made me wake up to the seriousness of the problem was one morning not long before a conference on climate change in Oxford, when I had to get up very early to go somewhere. The weather conditions were such that the sky was clear and the contrails very distinct against the blue. And I counted seventeen in the sky over my house – seventeen, and that was rural Oxfordshire. I thought: all of that stuff is going on all the time, this is just unsustainable, it really can't go on. That was a wake-up moment. But there are things to be done about it – this is not saying that we are utterly doomed, it's saying that we're doomed unless we look after ourselves, and we can do that.

In my trilogy, *His Dark Materials*, the characters discover a way of cutting through from one universe to another, and at the end of the first book, there's an explosion that rents the sky wide open. It wasn't a completely unconscious echo. I've been aware of the terms 'global warming' and 'climate change' for as long as they've been around. Unfortunately, unlike the characters in my story, we've only got one universe to play with, we can't skip through a hole into another one.

Of course, there is the danger of becoming didactic. Having a theme and then making up a story to fit it is the wrong way round. I don't know what the theme of a story is until I'm part way through it, and then it might turn out to be quite different from what I thought it was, which is fun. But you have to be surprised. If a story or a film or a play or any narrative is going to have any life, if it is going to affect people emotionally, it has to come from that part of you which doesn't think.

I believe we should begin young with storytelling. We should encourage teachers to tell stories – I don't mean read from a book, I mean tell from memory, and I don't mean reciting parrot-fashion either – I mean having the story securely in your head till you know it as well as you know your own address and phone number. Every young student I have taught, I have encouraged to do this. They were very nervous about it at first, because having a book in your hand is safe, you can rely on it, it does the memorizing for you – and if the lesson doesn't work, you can blame the book, you can hide behind it: the book is protection. But if you put the book away and it's just you in front of a class of children, in front of those thirty pairs of eyes, then you do feel very naked, very vulnerable at first. And all of them who did it said, 'Well, it really worked, I was amazed!'

'They weren't looking at me, they were looking at the story', somebody said. Every teacher should have room in their heads to carry one story for each week of the school year. So that, at the drop of a hat, fifteen minutes before the final bell goes, or whatever it might happen to be, they can tell a story, without preparation or props. Nothing else, just 'Sit down, I'm going to tell you a story.' And the kids would love it. That kind of storytelling, in that setting, would do an enormous amount of good. And so would nursery rhymes for very young children. If you see a young child of eighteen months or one year sitting on a parent's or grandparent's lap, playing clapping games and finger games and tapping out the rhythm of 'The grand old Duke of York, he had 10,000 men', you know that child will have a feeling for language that tells them that language is fun, that language is to be played with, language is safe, I can do funny things with language, I can enjoy the sound it makes without worrying about the meaning. It's a predictor of success like no other.

Something else which is very salient is the fragmentation of family life. Especially when every member of the family has their own i-pod, their own computer, games console, and television, and they don't exist as a unit at all, except by virtue of living in one house, they all go off and do their own things, they don't talk. Most of their attention is not devoted to the unit, to the maintenance of the happiness of the unit, of the group, it's devoted to the gratification of themselves alone. And I think that's awful.

Q: What gives you a sense of well-being?

If I ask myself, what is the thing that gives me a sense of well-being, my first answer would have to be, a good day's work. If I have done my thousand words, my three pages, and it's gone well, then nothing else matters – I'm satisfied. If I've done it, and it's gone badly, well, I can correct it tomorrow, it's there. If I combine that with a little bit of exercise, a little bit of play, which for me involves usually making things with wood, or playing music, and if my family is well and happy, and I have something nice to eat – that would be a good day for me.

I am very lucky. And I'm wary of preaching about how we should live, because I know how lucky I am: very few people have the chance to do what they want to do and stop when they want to stop doing it, and I do. Mind you, for thirty years I didn't. I had to work – to write – in my spare time while I was doing other jobs. So, actually, perhaps I am entitled to preach a little bit. So I'm entitled to say that in order to do the thing you want to do then you have to do it, whether or not you've got the time, and if it means missing *Neighbours*, then miss *Neighbours* or *EastEnders* or whatever. You must ask, which is more important to you in the end?

I also like using tools and making things out of wood. At the moment I'm making a rocking horse, and I've been making it for about two years now. It's in its final shaping stage, I've just got a bit of shaving off its rather fat rump. I used poplar wood for the head and the neck. It's quite soft and easy to carve. The legs are made of ash because they will take a lot of strain, and ash is a strong, springy wood. And soon I shall paint it, and then put it on a stand. That should be quite easy to make because it's just joinery, no carving involved. And then it'll be ready for my grandchildren, who have been saying impatiently, 'Grandpa, do some more horse!'

Q: Have you done anything to reduce your own environmental impact?

Around the house, all our light bulbs apart from the ones in the kitchen are low energy ones. In the kitchen there are these bloody halogen things. We had our kitchen done three or four years ago, I said, 'We want low energy lights' and the designer said, 'Oh, these are low energy.' Well, they're not, actually, they're 50 watts each. What he meant was they're low voltage, which isn't the same thing. We seldom have the central heating up high, because neither of us likes being particularly hot. The real problem is cooling down in the summer. It's an old house with quite thick walls, so it could be worse, but what I want to do, apart from putting solar panels on the roof, is to put an awning up outside the bedroom so that it doesn't heat up too much during the day. I've thought about a wind turbine, but it's a question of effectiveness. There isn't a clear place for it anywhere. In principle, I'd have everything, I'd plaster the house with photovoltaic cells and have wind turbines off every gable.

I've cut out international travel as much as possible. That wasn't hard to do because I hate flying. But I've got to go to America later this year in connection with books and films. I say I've got to, but I suppose I could say 'No'. I don't feel too guilty about electricity because we buy it from Good Energy, which supplies it from renewable sources. So I don't feel too bad when I'm playing my electric guitar.

Q: You have said that, as a writer, you are interested in the shape of things, what do you think is the shape of a good life?

What do we mean by 'a good life'? Do we mean a life that is pleasant and satisfying, which is what we normally mean by a good life, or a life full of moral purpose? We might mean the latter. But the two cross over. It would be nice to think that such a life would be available to everyone, but the shapes our lives take vary enormously.

The shape of a life seen from the inside is not necessarily the same as the same life seen from outside. There are several aspects to this question. One is that your life is not the same as your life story. Your life begins when you are born, obviously, but your life story begins in your teens, because that's the time when you begin to decide who you are. You measure yourself against your family, usually to their discredit, and decide that you can't possibly have been born to these people. You must be a changeling, and you belong somewhere better, where people treat you with courtesy and respect.

Everybody goes through this in adolescence, when they try to find out who they are. And that's when your story begins. And it might be an exciting story or a dull story, or it might be a story that finishes very early. For example, the life story of a footballer might begin in his teens. But that story will end in his mid-thirties, or earlier if he is unlucky. And he might be a fantastic player, he might win the premiership, play for England, score the winning goal in the World Cup Final. But as far as the world is concerned, his story will end when he retires, although his life goes on, of course.

And you can get the opposite of that, for example, somebody like Joan of Arc, whose life ended at the age of eighteen, but whose life story went on developing and growing and it wasn't until 500 years later that she was canonized. Life stories and lives don't overlap, that's one thing. The other thing is that a life may be very satisfying from within but seem pretty tedious from without. Or alternatively it may be full of anguish from within, but from the outside it may look inspirational. So lives, and the shapes of lives, and life stories and their shapes, depend very much on where you are seeing them from.

The challenge of having to change behaviour so that good lives don't have to cost the Earth goes deeper than having the right aspirational model. It goes right back into evolutionary psychology. I think we're made in such a way, we've evolved in such a way, that suits conditions on the savannah 500,000 years ago. We evolved to suit a way of life which is acquisitive, territorial, and combative.

The degree to which the processes of civilization, or socialization, can overcome that depends on the timescale. In the short term I feel pessimistic about it, because, civilization has had a very, very short time, only about 6,000 years, to overcome the millions of years of evolution.

So, I don't see much sign that enlightened tolerance, kindness and sweetness of nature is increasingly widespread among mankind. But in the long term I back evolution – if we survive this crisis that we're in. I was reading James Martin's book *The Meaning of the 21st Century* recently. His point was that we are approaching a crisis. It's like going down a river, approaching the rapids, and about mid-century we're going to go through the rapids, and it's going to be terribly difficult for all of us. But we can survive, and if we can get through this, he says, it's going to be wonderful.

Q: How do you strike the right balance between telling people the difficult truth about environmental problems, and still making them feel that it's worth getting out of bed in the morning to tackle them?

Frightening people is a very good way to make them passive and supine. You can be terrified into an abject denial of everything and you don't want to know about it, you just shut your eyes and your ears. But the most useful, the most helpful and most energizing thing is to say 'You can do this, and this, and this, and you can press your Government to do that.'

Environmentalists need to know something about basic storytelling in order to make their words effective. Samuel Johnson apparently said something I find very useful to remember: 'The true aim of writing is to enable the reader better to enjoy life, or better to endure it.' Research is much easier than writing, so you do a lot of research and then you reluctantly take up your pen, or turn on your computer, and start by saying 'Once upon a time there was'. But the temptation is of course to shove all the research in, because you've found it so interesting, and you're sure the readers will find it interesting too. But page after page after page of the stuff goes by and of course they stop reading. So you've got to be ruthless. The function of research is not to put it in the book but to enable you to make up the stuff you don't know.

I suppose the real story, the basic story, the story I would like to hear, see, read, is the story about how connected we are not only with one another but also with the place we live in. And how it's almost infinitely rich, but it's in some danger; and that despite the danger, we can do something to overcome it. People feel helpless when they see pictures of devastated forests cut down and the glaciers melting and the poor polar bear sweating on its bare rock in the sea. 'What can we do, what can we do?' People need to be told what it is that they can do. And they also need to feel that civil action, civil society, civil forms of involvement such as Parliament, local councils and so on, are there for a purpose and should be used, can be influenced.

There's a real disconnection now between the political process and most people, which is why the numbers of people voting is going down and down and down. People feel first, it doesn't make any difference. Secondly, they don't trust politicians, they think they're all in it for themselves. And thirdly they think 'I'm not interested, it's all boring.' And politicians in this country, and probably in most countries, certainly in the States, have got in on a minority of those voting. So a part of dealing with this is changing the electoral system; we need to have a more just, fairer, more representational Parliament, which means being proportional. They went ahead with it for the Scottish Parliament and the Welsh Assembly. So in principle there is no reason why they shouldn't have it for Westminster, and I think a proportional system of election would engage people a little more, which in turn might encourage them to think that politicians can be influenced a little more, which can only be a good thing. This disconnection is very bad between the actors on the political stage and the people who feel themselves to be in the audience and not connected with it.

Q: Taking a step back, how do you feel about life at the moment?

Thinking about well-being, right now, I'm feeling pretty good; my health is intact; my family is all intact; my work is going reasonably well. It never goes entirely smoothly, the work, because there are too many things which can go wrong and do go wrong, but then you know you can fix them. It's a continual challenge and a continual interest and a continual – well, an occasional pleasure.

I find myself at the age of sixty quite unexpectedly rich. My mind boggles, because I've been very poor most of my life. My childhood was formed during the austerity years after the war. So I still feel influenced by that. Curious, isn't it, we were much healthier as a nation after the war when the rationing was on. In a sense it was easier then because everybody knew there was a war on; you didn't get people like Melanie Phillips or Dominic Lawson saying 'War? Of course there isn't a war. It's just a conspiracy to get money out of us. All the scientific evidence is forged. Real scientists know there isn't any such thing as a war.'

Q: Talk to me about polar bears. Their perilous fate has become symbolic of global warming, but you also give them a hard time in your own books. . .

The armoured bears in my trilogy survive. Just. I've got a soft spot for them. I expect many of us have; those who haven't been eaten by one. It was in Edinburgh zoo that I first became emotionally affected by polar bears. It was a hot day, and the bear was just stretched out on the concrete, in a little pen no bigger than this room. I thought, 'This is absolutely monstrous!' An animal like that wants the ice, wants 50,000 square miles to roam about in. It's worse than slavery – absolutely appalling to keep an animal in those conditions. This one was lying there looking as though it wished it was dead.

Now, they're all going to be extinct if there's no ice left, unless they put them all in zoos or round them up and put a fence round them and throw them a seal or two from time to time. But that's no life.

If the polar bears leapt from the pages of my fiction into reality and saw what was happening, they'd eat us. Eat as many of us as quickly as they possibly could. And good luck to them.

Q: Do you think there might be a less carnivorous solution?

One less drastic solution we hear talk of, is a tradable carbon ration. If you have unused credit you can sell to somebody else. I think that's wrong. I think we should have a fixed limit and that's it. This is a crisis as big as war, and you couldn't trade your ration book in the wartime. You were allowed 3 ounces of butter a week or whatever and that was it. And this is what it should be like with carbon. None of this carbon trading. We should have a fixed limit and if you use it all up in October then tough, you shiver for the rest of the year.

That's what I reckon but it won't happen because governments are too feeble. Governments are feeble now because all the western governments have bought into this neo-liberal capitalist orthodoxy that market knows best. They grovel before this false god, the market. And the market bloody well doesn't know best, the market is what got us into this mess.

But people don't see that, because they've got a new car, a new television set, a new this and a new that, and it's very difficult. If anything will kill us, if anything will destroy us, capitalism will. Marx was absolutely right. His diagnosis was his remedy, his prescription wasn't, but his diagnosis was absolutely right, that the market system would destroy everything worth having. He has that wonderful sentence, 'All that is solid melts into air, all that is holy is profaned.' Every social bond, everything that we thought was firm and established, wiped away. It is wiped away by money, by the mighty force, this universal acid of the market system. Magnificent.

A.C. Grayling

The Good Life:
Its Costs and its Profit

There are as many different kinds of possible good lives as there are individuals to have them. That is a forgotten truth in a world where just a few models of good lives are repeatedly offered for public consumption in advertising, films and television. There are in fact two basic such models, both premised on possession of enough money to make them possible.

One is the life of fashion, partying, luxurious recreation, achievement of appearance and style recognized by others as enviable, ownership of desirable branded objects, and celebrity.

The other is the life of easeful retirement from the world of bustle, competition and stressful demands, in a place and in a manner that evinces the same underlying presence of money as in the first model, but much more quietly, without the metropolitan bustle and whirl, and far from the admiring envy of onlookers.

The clearest depictions of both models are to be found in glossy magazines, many films, and some television soap operas, but most of all advertising, that mirror of dreams. A caricature example would have a beautiful and beautifully-attired woman step elegantly from a gleaming limousine on to a red carpet leading into a palatial hotel where a reception is in process for what one is led to assume is a celebrity throng. On the wrist of her handsome beau, who opens the car door for her, is a very expensive watch; or on her throat glow emeralds or diamonds; or perhaps it is the car itself that draws the devouring eyes of the crowd kept back, behind a barrier, from access to the life that this vignette proposes. For the attractiveness of this model, as with the alternative retirement model, is the exclusivity conferred by the power to consume overabundantly.

In both models what lifts people on to these planes of satisfaction is wealth, and wealth has become even more the sign of success, achievement and arrival – and not just in advanced Western countries – than it was in the past, when other signs, such as public recognition for achievement in the arts or sciences, or for getting to the top of a mountain, were equally or more important. Those sorts of achievement usually only get their due now when they can be turned into cash, as when the mountaineer can endorse a washing-powder on television, or a scientist can patent a widget and make a fortune.

The point of these remarks is to imply a reservation about the narrowing of models of good lives to a conception of them which makes 'the good life' mean, more or less, partying and fun, as opposed to meaning 'life that is worthwhile and flourishing'. Partying and fun are surely a component of good lives in this latter more earnest sense, and they are not to be sniffed at; but they are not the whole story, and in particular they are the wrong story if that is all that people mean by 'the good life'. Apart from anything else, making well-lived life synonymous with either of the two advertising-inspired models is too costly: both in terms of the disappointment it invites in personal experience, and in terms of the fact that it requires what has come to haunt the world: excessive consumption and production, waste, and relentless economic growth at the expense of the environment and human health.

A lesson in this respect is starkly offered by contemporary China, already an economic giant and continuing to grow like Topsy. Some commentators say that the main motivation for China's headlong developmental rush is determination to become a regional and eventually global hegemony, in imitation of the present United States, with mighty armed forces to underpin and sustain the role. Since only economic might can provide a platform for the realization of this dream, China has opened all throttles to attain it. And they have chosen to make the country rich in the currently classical manner of making its inhabitants rich. It is one of the great ironies of the age that it should be the Communist Party of China which has recreated in our time the unbridled capitalism that was instrumental to the United States' first burst of economic growth in the nineteenth century: but so it is.

In pursuit of their dream of national wealth the Chinese exemplify the cost all too readily incurred in doing so. They have wholly ignored environmental considerations and the health and safety of workers, and part of their economy uses forced labour in the immense gulag of detention camps in its south-western and western provinces. (Almost everyone in the West at least once a week touches something made by slave labour in China – a pair of plastic chopsticks, paper packaging, a hair-grip.) Some of the environmental disasters in China have been too serious to be contained by the usual blanket secrecy imposed by the Beijing authorities. Overwhelming pollution of the Songhua River in Heilongjiang Province early in 2007 and the bird flu epidemic of 2006 in Guangdong Province are just tips of an iceberg in what is estimated to be hundreds of billions of dollars worth of clean-up required by half a century of unrestrained and unregulated mining, agriculture and industrial activity which has proceeded without a moment's thought for environmental protections of any kind.

As the environment has suffered in pursuit of wealth – the wealth that would bring to the Chinese the dream of the limousine, the emerald necklace, the watch on the beau's wrist – so have the workers. Every week for all the years of the People's Republic of China's existence, men have died in the thousands of mines (more of them open every week) that produce the coal that burns unfiltered and pollutingly in the power stations that keep the factories working that pour out the goods that spread cheaply across the world to bring in the trade dollars that add to the country's burgeoning reserves.

Of course there is nothing wrong with a country growing rich by making and trading and succeeding in world markets: all that is admirable. But it is the unheeding cost to the environment and human well-being paid by China's rush to developed-world status that prompts anxiety. For of course, all it is doing is reprising what the West itself did and in too many respects is still doing: paying an exceedingly high price to pursue the dream of a good life that is, in reality, only a two-dimensional and partial form of such a thing, because it is focused so exclusively on repeated consumption and possession of goods and services.

Just as partying and fun are components of any life that is good to live, so too of course are beautiful clothes, and holidays, and comfortable attractive homes – no one would deny this. But there is a small voice whispering in the background of depictions of lives that appear good as measured by the number and type of possessions in them. What it whispers is a reminder that the value of such things is instrumental: they are helps to enjoyment, pleasure, and satisfaction – in other words, to those quite intangible things called emotional states. It is the quality of the emotional tenor of a life that makes it good or bad; bad if it is scarred by unhappiness, grief, failure, bitterness, good if it is illuminated by love, attainment, affirmation and respect from people one respects.

But material possessions are not the only helps to the emotional states that make life seem good, and in fact might not always be the best such helps. People have been happy with nothing but a rag and a dry place to sleep under a tree. But people are not wrong when they link wealth, or at least sufficiency of income, to good lives. This is because money buys a degree of autonomy, of independence, of self-government; and it is this that is essential to the good life. To live according to the wishes of others, to be a football in someone else's game, cannot eventually satisfy, because the life thus lived is not one's own choice, it is not the life built and directed by oneself. It is the fact of living in a way one has chosen for oneself that ultimately makes it good – or to put it another way: that ultimately makes it happy.

The reason for this, in turn, is that chosen lives are made out of chosen things: friends, occupations, places, the minutiae of daily existence, all as things selected from among options, and selected because there was a reason for choosing them. A prisoner in a dungeon has to accept having almost everything thrust upon him at the dictate of others; the free individual is the person who is in the opposite case.

A critic of these thoughts might point out that there are many people who would prefer the prisoner's situation to the free person's, because the agony of choice, the dilemma presented by too many options, is a tiresome and troubling thing. This is true: but very few dispassionate judges would think that the prisoner's life could count as good merely because his laziness was indulged by it.

The point of insisting on the fact that good lives are chosen ones, constituted by emotional states engendered by the outcome of that choosing, is that they do not have to cost very much. Reflection on what is involved in either of the models of the good life that we daily see on large and small screens illustrates a mismatch between what actually makes people feel that their lives are good, and the standard images of what good lives look like. Ask anyone what would give more enduring grounds for the emotional sense that life is good, and they will come up with a familiar list, very little of which involves much cost, if any, either to the environment or to human health. This is, in fact, very well known; there are a thousand clichés available to remind us that money and possessions do not yield more than temporary happiness, that true wealth lies in such intangibles as health and love, and so on: we all know the mantras, and yet, at the same time, the shops are full of people buying, and glossy magazines and television advertisements continue to purvey their glamorous theories about the marks of social and personal success.

It is worth repeating that there is nothing wrong with the lovely things one can buy to wear or do, unless one imagines that they are ends in themselves rather than instrumental to something more worth having, which is attainment of the emotional sense that life is good. Retail therapy can have that effect, for sure, because it is not called so for nothing; but in the course of a lifetime it is only going to be a sporadic and occasional aid, and since it is not the final answer it invites the question: is the process by which the means for retail therapy are provided (i.e. the industrial behemoth that is devouring our Earth, its seas and trees and air), in their current form anyway, really worth it in light of the fact that this is not where final happiness lies?

Oliver James

Houses Built on Sand

The Affluenza Virus is the placing of too high a value upon money, possessions, appearances (physical and social) and fame. Infection replaces our true needs with confected wants. We need emotional security or to be part of a community, we only want a newer i-pod or car. In no single domain is this better illustrated than that of property ownership and home improvement.

More than anything else, our personal finances are dominated by the 'need' to pay the mortgage on a residence whose purchase price is nearly always many times greater than our true means. The insatiability of the Virus means that, as well as having mortgaged ourselves to the limit, we never seem to be content with what we have, although for many of us a less expensive home would be perfectly adequate to meet our needs. There is always a better house, whether in a more fashionable area or street; we constantly hanker to improve what we have, the conservatory, the new kitchen or the sculpted garden; we may seek a second home and, on getting it, soon want a better one; even those who have acquired more homes than any individual could possibly need are liable to desire still more or better ones. We talk of 'needing' these things, but really, we only want them.

In Britain, the possession of homes as a source of status is nothing new. Until recently I had a variant of a recurring dream, one which doubtless says a lot about me but also illustrates just how profoundly the middle classes' inner lives have long been affected by property prices, albeit increasingly so in recent decades. Some preliminary explanation of my property history is required to make this dream intelligible to the reader.

In reality, rather than the dream, I used to own a rather beautiful two-bedroom flat in Notting Hill. It had high ceilings, and one very large room, and was similar in the grandeur of its stucco white exterior to one of the houses in which I was raised. We sold this flat when we moved to Shepherd's Bush, a cheaper nearby suburb, in order to afford a house with enough space for us to accommodate a family. This house is actually rather nice for what it is, with a largish hall, a quite spacious stairway with a bare pine wooden wall along one side of it. Even so, it is far less grand than the homes in which I was raised.

The basic gag in my recurring dream is that I purchase a second flat in Notting Hill, a very large one that I never actually occupy but bought as a property investment (this is something I would never have done in real life because I am not especially far-sighted, and in any case nowhere near rich enough). In the dream I have contrived to forget completely about the second flat, but on recalling its existence I pay a visit.

In various versions of the dream – it has been a bit like a soap opera in which there are plot developments each time – I have discovered that it has been rented out and that there is an extremely sinister man who now pretends to be its landlord. Further investigation, through the estate agent which markets it to potential renters, has revealed that it is now very valuable. However, I am powerless to realize my asset because I have lost the deeds, and anyway, when I confront the sinister man who pretends to be its owner, he subtly indicates that he will have me killed by a hit-man if I pursue my interest. In early versions of the dream I doubted that this was possible – surely people do not get rubbed out in this way? However, in succeeding dreams I have become convinced that this man really would do as he said, so I am powerless to realize my investment. In some dreams I have tried threatening the man so that he will at least share some of the large rents he is collecting with me, but always to no avail.

In last night's instalment, I was passing the flat and decided to investigate it again. I go up to the door and see a pair of potential renters being shown around it by a menacing thug employed by the impostor who is claiming to be the landlord. The thug slams the door in my face. Eventually I extract the particulars of the flat from one of the renters, and yet again am reminded of my predicament: I own a valuable flat but can do nothing to benefit from it. Yet again I threaten action, but the thug sees me off.

I need not trouble the reader with the myriad unconscious resonances that echo for me in this dream but I relate it as an example of how profoundly property dominates the lives of the British middle classes – it fills their very dreams. In my case, property has very particular associations, for it scarred the last decade of my father's life, as illustrated by a second recurring dream that I have. Again, before describing it I must crave your patience while I present some more biographical background.

My father's father, Warwick James, was a tyrannical, driven man, not averse to saying, 'Let's compromise and do things my way.' The son of a successful grocer in Northampton, he trained as a dentist and established a very fashionable practice in London, making enough money to rent two huge stucco-fronted houses overlooking Regent's Park (in Park Crescent).

His practice drew many of the rich and some of the famous of that era (at public school, my one claim to fame was that he did the teeth of Lawrence of Arabia – a pathetic brag, even for a schoolboy). For all his faults, Warwick was a dynamic man, the inventor of some of the equipment still used to this day to meddle with our teeth, and I believe he was also something of an expert in the field of physical anthropology, with a detailed

knowledge of the jaws of our ancestors. He was also a mountaineer, perhaps styling himself as a gentleman explorer. In his
old age he paid a heavy price for his pretensions, because he
had never actually purchased his homes. In order to live in
ones normally occupied by the aristocracy or successful busi-
nessmen, he had rented; when the lease became due, in his
mid-eighties, he could no longer afford to live there. He was
forced to vacate the premises and to move to a more modest
residence in Taunton, Somerset, where he eventually died.

Considering that my father was a psychoanalyst, analysed
by no less a figure than Freud's daughter Anna, you might
suppose that he would have avoided following in his father's
footsteps. Unfortunately, Anna Freud was not a terribly good
analyst. It seems unlikely that she ever had a sexual relationship, despite being a very vigorous proponent of her father's
famously sex-dominated theory. (She does seem to have had
some knowledge of sex, though. My dad once told me that he
had been going to his analysis with her when he felt an inex-
plicable urge to leap over the garden wall outside her house;
when he told her this, she asked, 'And did you have an erec-
tion at that moment?', which he did – God knows how she
could have surmised this if she had never seen an erect
penis.) Sadly, my dad contrived to repeat his father's dire
property error.

In 1967 he sold our freehold property in Knightsbridge and
bought a tremendously grand home nearby. The new house
was every bit as splendid as the one in which he had been
raised himself, even more so, but the trouble was that it had
only a 21-year lease. To be fair, at that time the 'charity' that
owned it seems to have been largely serving the purpose of
providing cut-price accommodation to the rich, although its
stated aim was to raise money for the poor. My father reasonably assumed that when the lease became due he would have
to pay only a small amount to renew it.

However, in the early 1970s the charity altered that policy and he was given three months to pay a substantial sum if he wished to renew the lease for a much longer term, after which the sum would rise even further. Perhaps he could have just afforded the new lease if he had sold his second home in Cornwall and every share he owned, but, never a worldly man, more a scholar, he did not do so – with grim consequences. As the end of the twenty-one years approached, he suffered terrible anguish, some of which he shared with me. Eventually, just as his father had done, he was forced to sell the rump of the lease and move to some far more modest lodgings (the extremely noisy Earls Court Road, no less).

I am sure that this explains why he was so unhappy in his final years. Having to go down in the property world was painful to him because, again oddly for a psychoanalyst, a good deal of his self-esteem rested upon living in a posh house, a prize-hunting pillar in the psyche of an otherwise vocal, and usually exceptionally convincing, advocate of the non-material in life. Furthermore, I am sure that he felt a failure for having lost a considerable sum of money through his dealings. (I am not alone in having had a father who made this mistake; when I did a newspaper interview with Sir John Harvey-Jones, the enlightened business guru, he told me that his father was 'the only man to have managed to lose money in the London property market'; I was able to assure him that he was not alone.)

Having risked the reader hurling the book down in disgust at all this autobiography, I can now recount my further recurring dream. My parents have sold our posh house but, mysteriously, my father is still living there because the new owners have only bought it as an investment and never bothered to live there or rent it out. My mother, meanwhile, has taken herself off to a new flat somewhere by the river. It seems that they are still perfectly affable in their dealings with each other but just prefer this arrangement. There have been many plot developments in this dream, but it is essentially a very sad one.

Of the numerous problems my dad suffered in his childhood, his father's social aspirations played a big role. My dad was sent to one of the most prestigious boarding private preparatory schools (i.e. for his primary education) of his era, St Cyprian's. Although I never discussed his time there with him (except that he said his life revolved around his personal Marmite jar, apparently a rare luxury permitted to the pupils in an otherwise Spartan regime), George Orwell described the place with characteristic lucidity in his essay 'Such, Such Were the Joys'. Orwell was a pupil there a few years before my dad (along with other famous artistic alumni, such as Cyril Connolly and Cecil Beaton). In Orwell's account, proximity to the royal family via aristocratic inheritance was a crucial determinant of how you were treated by the monstrous tyrant who ran the place.

Boys with a handle (The Hon., Lord, etc.) were pandered to, people like Orwell and my dad had to get by as best they could, a savage status system not based upon merit at all. Unlike most St Cyprian's graduates, my dad did not go to Eton but to Marlborough, a public school of lesser status. That he was not bound for Eton (and I wonder why not, given his father's contacts and social ambitions) was yet another sign of his inferiority. To top it all, dad went on to Magdalene College, Cambridge, which was then awash with Bertie Woosterish Old Etonians swanning about, apparently having a whale of a time.

Going back to my dream, it should be obvious from all this how my dad's sense of status might have become so strongly tied to his homes. Despite being a determined advocate of the importance of authenticity to fulfilment in life, and despite being highly skilled at nurturing it in his patients, he somehow contrived to be a property snob as well. He paid a very heavy price for this, in every sense. Meanwhile, my mum was much more mixed in her feelings about property. Also raised in grand residences, she had good reason to know that where you live has little to do with happiness. She always claimed she would be happy living in a council house (my father used to joke that 'she would get out of her Rolls-Royce to go and vote Labour'), although she did go along with dad's property adventures. So my dream is partly about the divide between them regarding the importance of your home as a sign of status: she moves out of our posh residence and into a more modest one.

The dream's wider significance is the way in which home ownership is easily confused with identity (a property fallacy). People whose childhoods leave them insecure are very vulnerable to it, and there are a lot of them. My dad was no dolt – far from it. He knew that outward signs of status cannot compensate for an inner sense of inadequacy. Yet even he fell into that trap, despite his impressive scientific and clinical understanding of precisely this issue when it came to his patients. His travails occurred before Thatcherism had created the massive gap between the richest and the poorest in Britain. Think how much greater the problem must be today, with its several hundred thousand more millionaires than in 1979, not to mention the large numbers of foreign investors in London property. Like my grandfather, some of these newcomers hail from relatively modest origins, and many have been motivated to succeed by insecurity-inducing childhood relationships with their parents. How easily must they unite the size, number and grandeur of their homes with their fragile identities?

John Bird

Who Needs Stuff?

I was born into a very violent kind of poverty, violent in every way imaginable: the family was violent, the neighbourhood was violent. It was a tough upbringing and generally very unforgiving. For example, if you don't pay your rent today, it's unlikely you'll get kicked out, or at least it's pretty hard to get rid of someone easily with all the legal protection that exists. But when I was growing up, if you didn't pay your rent, there was no safety net. That was it, bang, you were out on your ear. The world I grew up in was a violent, aggressive, wife-beating world. That was my own experience, but I'm not saying it was exclusive in any way to the working classes.

To me, it's not just about what makes a good life, but about the barriers that stand in the way of people getting there. The biggest of these is lack of hope. Social exclusion is one way of describing it, but it's a mind-set, really, caused by lack of hope.

The reasons people have a lack of hope are mainly cultural, and that's the thing we have to change. We have a large group of people in Britain who depend heavily on benefits and, as a result, whose life is essentially determined by other people. They never get the right kind of schooling or the right kind of social training. We, as a society, are servicing a deficit in their lives and, because of that, we never get a chance to help them escape from it.

In a way you could say there is nothing wrong with poverty, as long as there is a way out of it, as long as people can climb out of it. But in order to climb out of it, to gain some kind of social mobility, you need to create the kind of culture that helps build self-esteem and provides the necessary training.

Whereas what we've got is a very self-defeating social security system that guarantees dependence for far longer than people need it. In fact, if you slip into dependency, like a large number of my family have, it becomes a poisoned chalice. You get stuck there, and you stay there.

I work with homeless people. You can always tell a homeless person. They are the ones who don't get a choice. They get given the pullover that you don't want. They get the trousers that are no longer worn. They get the hostel bed that is assigned to them. They don't get what they want. They get what they are given.

Choice is the great decider. Cut out choice and you cut out democracy. And, unfortunately, the poorer you are the less chance you have of participating in democracy. So choice to me rings a kind of bell. If you limit choice, or someone decides what choice you can make, then it harms you. It limits you. And in the end it ensures that you feel limited by that experience.

What we need today is to keep monopolies out of our life. Whenever we have a monopoly, whether public or private, you have the limitation of choice. You have the dismantling of democracy. Don't kid yourself that monopolies are about the fair play of the market place. What a monopoly does is dismantle competition and ensure that you have only the choices that are imposed on you, by someone who controls the marketplace.

Without a healthy marketplace where genuine choice is made available, then the community itself shrivels up. The community becomes what the monopoly decides it should be. A monopoly doesn't have to listen to what you want. A monopoly in the end tells you what they will give you. Homeless people demand to get back into society so that they can start making choices. They want to mature their views on life. They don't want to be told their choices. Right or wrong, they want to make their own. But in order for that to happen, we need to encourage a single mother living on a council estate to have the same kind of engagement in politics and democracy that someone from a more educated, privileged background does.

I don't think it's so much that people are disillusioned with democracy and politics; it's just that they don't always see how their actions can make a direct difference. If you look at the areas where people are really involved in their local community, or at least local politics, it's often the nice, rich ones. So if the local council, or whoever, try to introduce something that's unpopular or not wanted, like a massive supermarket, the middle class residents kick up a massive fuss until something gets done about it. I'd like to see that kind of involvement from everyone, regardless of their background or where they live.

Looking back, in some ways my life was more hectic twenty years ago than it is now. I was running a printing business, travelling a lot, getting as many holidays as I could, always going out, looking for new things. I wasn't a particularly happy person then. My life has changed remarkably in that time. I'm very aware of the limitations of the planet. But also, I'm not into conspicuous expenditure. Somebody recently asked me what my carbon footprint was and I said I cycle, I hardly drive a car, I live in a small house, and I rarely go on foreign holidays. I'm not a traveller, if I go somewhere it's because I have to go there for work, and if I have a holiday, more often than not it's in England. I use local transport, I have a small television, I haven't got a plasma, I go to the cinema when I want to go out and when I do, I usually go by bike or bus.

The environment, in its widest sense, is very important for how we feel about things. I wanted to launch the wedge card as a way of supporting local shops and businesses, because they matter. They are, really, the things that hold our communities together, and if they start to disappear, which they are in a lot of places, then everything else starts to fall apart as well. Local shops and businesses generally make up some of the most important building blocks of where we live. I just don't understand how, for instance, you can have a 'local' supermarket – there's no such thing.

What makes me happy now? I draw, I go to the cinema, and I write all the time, I'm always in the middle of about three books. I read an awful lot in fact, but I don't take the daily papers, I just ask people what's going on. Why bother reading a paper when you can find out by talking to a real person? I find the papers are just so distorted in their delivery of the news, so I think increasingly, what is the point? And I don't really think it's important to know what Paris Hilton is doing, or where Madonna is travelling to now. It's just unnecessary information. I don't care about speculation, whether one person is more famous than the other, who the biggest celebrity is this week. It's really not important.

To me, a good life is a conscious life, one that is lived with awareness. Knowing what is the impact of the decisions you make and things you do, on other people. Too many people are stumbling through life in a trance, not really aware of what they're doing or why they're doing it.

How did I get out of poverty and get a good life? I started going out with middle class girlfriends, that's how.

3

Good Money

Imagine overhearing someone talking about the value of 'natural beauty', 'happiness', the threat of environmental crises, in the same breath as the 'confused economic concept of "competitiveness"', how we *can* allow population sizes in rich countries to reduce, and the need to 'dethrone growth' as the principle objective of the economy, who would you think was talking? Your first guess is unlikely to throw up the person's true identity. **Adair Turner**, who today is a non-executive director of Standard Chartered Bank, has come a long way since he was head of the famously hard-nosed Confederation of British Industry. Reading his tightly argued essay, few will doubt that we have to follow him on his journey.

As founder of The Body Shop, **Anita Roddick** was Britain's best known ethical businesswoman and sadly died while this book was being produced. Her contribution here is one of the last things she wrote. It captures the deeply personal nature of her engagement with the big issues of our time. She struggled for many years, and like few others, to put principles into practice. But her wake-up call to the scale of necessary change came in the form of some very nasty smelling salts wafted on a Seattle sea breeze. Anita attended the infamous meeting of the World Trade Organisation Organization in the American city towards the end of 1999. One day she was surrounded by 300 children dressed as turtles. It was a campaign to change trade rules in such a way that turtles would be less likely to get caught up in shrimp nets. The next day she was surrounded by 'police looking like storm-troopers, with gas masks, full body armour and jackboots'. In addition to the clouds of tear gas, there was, she said, also 'a great deal of blood'. She explains here how she found herself as the only chief executive of a major international retailer on the painful side of the police lines, and how that experience changed her life. She is missed.

Leading the Jubilee 2000 debt relief campaign, **Ann Pettifor** became an internationally known figure. As author of the *The Coming First World Debt Crisis*, she turns the mirror of reform on to the wealthy countries who are equally to blame for the debt crisis that still harms poor countries. How is it that we are so rich, asks Ann, but cannot afford the things that matter like providing schools, hospitals and environmental protection to those who need them? To pay for vital public and environmental works, she argues, there is no reason why publicly owned banks could not create debt-free money (i.e.: non-interest bearing). In this way, we would not have to depend on expensive private finance to pay for 'maternity wards, houses and the rainforest'. Using arguments earlier made by characters as diverse and unlikely as Henry Ford and President Lincoln, she is convinced that things are not set in stone, 'The world really does not have to be this way. We can change it.'

Larry Elliott is one of Britain's best known commentators on the economy. As economics editor of the *Guardian* newspaper and author of *Fantasy Island*, a book about the legacy of Tony Blair's ten years in power, and *The Age of Insecurity*, there are few aspects of national life that he has not analysed. Having done so, he returns to the mature wisdom of Charles Dickens's Mr Micawber who advises on the ease with which subtly different courses of action can result in either happiness or misery. The trick is, he says, to live within your means. Unfortunately, concludes Larry, 'Britain is a country that is living beyond its means at every level, personal, national and environmental.' At the heart of it, he writes, is a model of consumption, financed by debt, that should be exposed for what it is, 'the dodgiest sort of leveraged buy-out'. Sleep-walking into a warming world, we face the environmental equivalent of the Cuban missile crisis. Instead of the current economic system which 'operates on the basis that there is no such thing as enough', Larry argues that we need a 'prolonged period of restraint, moderation and thrift'.

Adair Turner

Dethroning Growth

Rising economic prosperity has delivered huge increases in human welfare. The fifteenfold increase in western living standards between 1800 and today has freed almost all people in the developed world from the burdens of grinding poverty and backbreakingly hard work. Life expectancy has soared, health has improved dramatically, and for the first time in human history the mass of ordinary people have come to enjoy significant leisure time during working life and retirement after it. Globalization of the free market system is increasingly spreading that prosperity, particularly in Asia: on World Bank estimates economic growth has lifted 400 million Chinese out of extreme poverty since 1980. Life expectancy in China has increased from about sixty-five in 1980 to about seventy-five today; in India infant mortality has halved in the last twenty-five years.

The local environmental impact of industrialization, urbanization and rising prosperity has in all cases been strongly adverse at first – late nineteenth-century London and today's Beijing both suffering terrible air pollution. Beyond a certain level of prosperity, however, people have demanded that technology is used to clean up their local air and rivers as well as to deliver them more material goods and services. One reason for rising life expectancy is that in some aspects environmental standards are also relentlessly rising.

But it is also true that rising prosperity has unleashed long term environmental harm. It has made possible a global population explosion from 1 billion in 1800 to 6.5 billion today, with growth to over 9 billion likely by 2050 and no certainty of stabilization thereafter. Local pollution problems may be solved by the application of the same technologies which drive economic growth, but at the global level that growing population, on average increasingly rich, is imposing an unsustainable burden on the world's environment. Increasing demands for fresh water are destroying fragile ecosystems and in some cases threaten conflict between nations.

The biodiversity of the planet is being eroded at an alarming rate. And man-made greenhouse emissions are changing the world's climate, with uncertain but potentially very harmful results. Prosperity itself indeed destroys some of the things that more prosperous people increasingly value. Once our basic needs are met, we increasingly value natural beauty and the tranquillity of unspoilt countryside, but rising prosperity and increasing population growth gradually destroy them.

Perhaps partly as a result of this, but also for more inherent reasons, the relationship between economic prosperity, as measured by GDP per capita, and human welfare or well-being, breaks down once a certain level of prosperity is reached. As Richard Layard shows in his recent book *Happiness*, the standard of living reached by the western world in say 1960 makes people happier than that of much of the Third World today, but beyond that level the link between rising material prosperity and human well-being is uncertain and at best weak.

Human beings inherently value freedom from hunger and physical insecurity, freedom from drudgery, the ability to enjoy some leisure time and a certain level of comfort, but there is no empirical basis for believing that the aggregate happiness of British people will increase significantly if British GDP per capita grows by 20 per cent over the next ten years. And there is a danger that increased material growth will directly generate effects that make some people unhappy: increased road traffic driving congestion, frustration and road rage; increased house prices driving anxiety among those not already on the housing ladder.

But the very fact that beyond a certain level increased prosperity does not drive increased happiness is in itself a clue to one step we should take to make it more likely that good lives do not cost the Earth – which is to dethrone the idea that maximizing the growth in measured prosperity, GDP per capita, should be an explicit objective of economic and social policy.

This does not imply that we can enthrone 'happiness' as the alternative explicit objective, confident that we know what public policy levers to pull to increase it. As Paul Ormerod has pointed out, while it is true that happiness is not correlated with rising prosperity beyond a certain level, there is also no clear correlation between happiness and many other possible policy objectives, such as reduced inequality. Nor does the dethroning of GDP per capita growth as an objective imply that economic growth should or will cease or even significantly slow down.

For it is highly likely that further steady increases in prosperity measured by GDP per capita will arise if other desirable ends are achieved. Reasonably full employment should be an end in itself because unemployment makes people unhappy. People who want to should be free to work hard and improve their income, because for some people that is important, and because if people are not able to compete to improve their relative position in legal and open ways, they are likely to do so in corrupt and harmful ways. Individuals who wish to innovate new technologies and new products should receive a reasonable reward for so doing, because innovation and creativity are in themselves attractive ends. If desirable features of a free society are in place, it is highly likely that a steady increase in measured GDP will naturally occur.

But it should occur as a by-product of these other desirable objectives, not, in already rich countries, as an end in itself. In poor African countries steady growth in GDP per capita should still be an important measure of good government. But the fact that one rich country has achieved a growth rate of 1.8 per cent per capita per annum while another 'languishes' at 1.6 per cent should ideally be largely irrelevant to political debate, since largely irrelevant to human welfare.

The need to maximise GDP per capita should therefore not be used as the clinching argument in debates over alternative social policies. The merits of further out-of-town retail development should be debated locally and in the light of specific local advantages and disadvantages without reference to a supposed national imperative to improve national productivity. The pros and cons of further road development, or of tighter environmental standards, should be debated without introducing a confused economic concept of 'competitiveness', which mistakenly asserts that we cannot choose to sacrifice a sliver of future GDP per capita growth without risking an actual fall in prosperity and employment in the face of low wage competition. And if one country falls behind another in GDP per capita not because it has higher unemployment, or less freedom to innovate, but simply because its citizens choose to take the benefits of new technology in more leisure not more material consumption, that should be welcomed for its beneficial impact on environmental sustainability, not denigrated as an unaffordable choice.

Dethroning the maximization of measured GDP as an end in itself is particularly important in relation to the two greatest and interrelated environmental challenges – climate change and population growth. Nick Stern's review of *The Economics of Climate Change* has argued that the costs of significantly mitigating climate change are far less than the potential adverse consequences, but it is important to understand that Stern's estimate of those adverse consequences, at an equivalent of 5–20 per cent of global GDP, depends on placing a value on key elements of human welfare, such as freedom from disease, which do not automatically show up in formal measures of GDP. And Stern himself stresses that this 'equivalent percentage of GDP' approach should only be used to complement an approach to climate change policy decisions in which people directly consider the different human and ecological consequences of climate change, rather than seek a single measure whose maximization provides the answer.

As for Stern's estimate, confirmed by many other economists, that the costs of significantly mitigating climate change are likely to be at most a few percentage points of global GDP, the argument that this is very small compared to the potential adverse consequences becomes even more compelling once the lack of correlation between measured GDP and human happiness is considered. Even if the cost of mitigating climate change for rich developed countries was as much as 5 per cent of GDP, this would simply mean that measured economic prosperity would have to wait till mid-2052 to reach the level it might otherwise have reached by January 2050, a level likely to be about twice current levels. Given that there is no strong correlation between GDP per capita growth and human well-being, even this much higher cost than Stern has estimated could not be considered as a conclusive argument against action.

Population stabilization will be crucial to our long term success in dealing with climate change and other global environmental impacts. However much we reduce our environmental impact per capita, the effect of this will be outweighed if the world population grows in perpetuity. Rising material prosperity has been the driver of the world's population explosion; but it is also crucial to the solution. Material prosperity drives population explosion as the harmful by-product of the wonderful achievement of lower infant and child mortality. But it is close to a global rule that wherever three things are achieved – high female literacy, at least a modicum of economic growth, and a legal supply of contraceptives – fertility rates fall to and usually below replacement level.

In still poor parts of the world, therefore, material economic growth, while sometimes adverse for the environment in the short term, is essential to the attainment of population stabilization, without which long term environmental sustainability will never be permanently achieved. In the developed world, however, the key challenge is to reject the confused arguments increasingly used to portray population stabilization as a problem which must be reversed rather than a natural and welcome development.

What is true is that extremely low birth rates, sustained over the long term, would create problems. Italy's fertility rate of 1.4 children per woman, if permanently maintained and if not offset by immigration, would place enormous strains on the affordability of Italy's pension system. But rich developed countries are quite capable of living with fertility rates slightly below 2 and thus with gently declining populations. A rising proportion of older people in the population is manageable provided countries make sensible reforms to pension systems, increasing retirement ages in line with life expectancy. And the effects of demographic slowdown on GDP growth should not worry us provided we are clear about appropriate objectives.

The fact that the growth of total UK or total European GDP will be diminished if the population grows more slowly is obvious but utterly irrelevant, since human welfare is not enhanced by a larger national or continental economy. The fact that population stability or slight decline may, as a result of the lower proportion of workers in the population, have a mildly negative effect on the growth of GDP per capita, is worth noting. But since GDP per capita maximization should not be the overriding objective, it is not a sound basis on which to cast population stabilization as a problem rather than a welcome development.

Rising prosperity and rising population have been the distinctive features of the last millennium and in particular the last 300 years of human history, first in western Europe and its offshoots, then later in the rest of the world. In the 700 years before 1700, by contrast, little such growth occurred, and in the first millennium of the post-Christian era hardly any. That increased prosperity has delivered huge human welfare benefits, and its further progress is essential to lift more people out of poverty. But further growth will inevitably have a huge environmental effect and ensuring that it does not cost the Earth will not be easy. Whether we can achieve economic growth in Africa early enough and fast enough to stabilize the population at a sustainable level is unclear.

Achieving agreement on a global approach to climate change is essential, but will be very difficult. But one thing we can do to make success more likely is to avoid being guided by misleading objectives. Increasing human welfare in already rich countries does not depend on maximizing measured GDP per capita, even though further growth is the likely consequence of other desirable objectives. And increasing human welfare will be made more likely if we welcome population stabilization as the desirable by-product of increasing prosperity, rather than rejecting it in the pursuit of the even more irrelevant objective of growth in absolute national GDP.

Dame Anita Roddick

On the Painful Side of the Line

> If I had the power today, I should most deliberately set out to endow our capital cities with all the appurtenances of art and civilization on the highest standards ... convinced that what I could create I could afford – and believing that money thus spent would not only be better than any dole, but would make unnecessary any dole. For what we have spent on the dole in England since the war we could have made our cities the greatest works of man in the world.
>
> John Maynard Keynes, 'National Self-sufficiency', 1933

It is nearly a decade since I was tear-gassed in a Seattle street, a strange situation for the CEO of one of the biggest retailers in the world. It was a formative experience that made me realize one or two important things about the world.

It was the end of November 1999, and I was in the city, together with thousands of others, for what proved to be the failed summit of the World Trade Organization. One day, there were 300 children dressed as turtles, a reference to the WTO decision that it was illegal to discriminate against shrimps caught in nets that also drown 150,000 sea turtles. The next day, and I was suddenly witnessing scenes I had never encountered before. There was tear gas everywhere, rubber bullets fired point blank into crowds of demonstrators, pepper spray, and police looking like storm-troopers, with gas masks, full body armour and jackboots, and without visible badges or forms of identification. There was also a great deal of blood.

What seemed particularly unjust was that, as far as I know, there was no property destruction or violence before this violence, except that the delegates had been prevented from entering the Convention Centre and the Paramount Theatre, where the opening ceremonies were supposed to be held. It was unnerving watching tear gas and rubber bullets used against students, their professors, clergy, Tibetan monks, even medical staff alike. Scrambling for safety as the pepper spray hit us, choking on the smell of cayenne pepper that sticks to everything, I grabbed the environmentalist Paul Hawken, and found we were both temporarily blinded, with burning faces, stumbling between other protestors, as we searched for water.

The whole experience of being tear-gassed in Seattle changed my life. For one thing, I realized I was probably the only chief executive of a major international retailer on that side of the police cordons, and that made me feel worried – not for me but for the business world. Being a successful entrepreneur is about imagining the world differently: if the only ones who succeed in doing so side with the powerful, then something is wrong. For another thing, I realized also that the people behind that kind of globalization would really stop at nothing to impose their will on the world.

Because there is more than one kind of globalization.

I mean that I am still overwhelmingly in favour of a sense of the planet that is aware of the multiplicity of cultures and respects them, can see into the dark corners and reveal the cruelties going on there – can even do something about them. But the side of globalization peddled then by the WTO, and taken to a whole new level since by the Bush administration, is that only money and power matter – and that, somehow, the exercise of both will filter down and help the poorest people of the world.

Being in Seattle, trying to find vinegar and water for my smarting eyes, made me horribly aware of this rogue globalization and what it meant.

But in the years that followed, Seattle came to mean something else to me. It was the turtles, fancy dress, costumes, colour and music, and the sense of carnival. The sheer joy of it. It was a valiant attempt, not just to seize the streets in a crude pretence at power, but to humanize that vision of raw power with creativity, imagination and fun.

Most corporations are in two minds about the whole idea of carnival. They like a sense of occasion because they can sell greetings cards, fizzy drinks and gifts. But, equally, they tend to be afraid of this creative power that people have, of people taking their own initiative, and they share the fear that governments have always had of what they call 'the mob', of people taking their own decisions, or doing almost anything in the street except shopping or commuting to work.

Neither of those are necessary in themselves for people to lead fulfilled lives; joy, colour and a sense of occasion are vital and – most of all – so is beauty. People have a range of needs to live a reasonable life, and often it may be more obvious to them what makes them *unhappy* than what makes them happy. If they feel isolated, unappreciated, insecure materially and socially, or simply unloved, they will be unhappy. But it is more complicated than that: the evidence suggests that they are more miserable when they live in a society where there is a huge gap between the rich and the poor, when life and society make no sense, or where they have less influence in their political life.

On the other hand, we know that people thrive on love and intimacy within the family and trust and care within the community. Abraham Maslow's Hierarchy of Needs suggests that we grow from the simple fulfilling of basic needs – food and warmth – to find fulfilment in sharing, even in sacrifice, and to find joy in the community and creativity. The consumer society provides little of either. It has even been suggested that the consumer society keeps everyone in perpetual infancy because, if they ever became satisfied with their material lives, they would cease to play the game of expanding desires that keeps the perpetual economy going.

Consumerism prevents the possibility of fulfilling those higher needs. It doesn't care whether we buy in beautiful or ugly surroundings. Few aspects of the global economy that we were all tear-gassed in the name of provide beauty or community and, worse, in many ways the global economy drives them out by the deliberate manipulation of debt, which is as powerful a motivator – as powerful a tyranny – as any invented in human history. On the other hand, providing for these vital human needs requires another kind of economy altogether, which emphasizes beauty, community and creativity.

So let's imagine, for a moment, that beauty is the central plank in the Government's new manifesto. Let's go further, and imagine myself sworn in as a Government minister charged with responsibility for public space.

The first thing I would discover once I was behind my Whitehall desk was that the job wouldn't just be fun, it would be really inexpensive. The first thing I would do is to organize a Day of Common Delight, an annual carnival of beauty which can turn the world upside-down, as they did in the Middle Ages. The second item on the agenda would be to draft a new law for billboards. They would no longer be allowed to sell products; only poetry, wit and art would be allowed.

That should take the first few days. After that, it's a matter of getting waterproofed pianos, also theft proof, to arrive quietly in public squares, and fields. Then there would be the legislation to draft to allow Italian Pavement Art Day, Art Car Days, where you can decorate your car any way you want – covered in grass, or emblazoned with thousands of pieces of cut glass, or covered in cake.

In fact, my work as minister of state is made much easier because the traditional notion of public art – some discreet object made without much consideration for a particular place – is already undergoing a transformation. Artists seem much more aware of what it means to work in the community, increasingly in prisons or schools or among the homeless. I have seen death row art, prison art where the artist plays the role of a facilitator, helping to draw forth the stories.

Sometimes you barely need an artist at all. I remember travelling by tube from Victoria recently, and as I entered the train, someone sabotaged the loudspeaker system and sang 'Hey, ho, hey ho, It's off to work we go . . . !' Commuters burst out laughing, and looked at reactions from others, and it was rather an amazing transformation: the community of commuters finally having fun.

As minister in charge of public space, I would put myself alongside the work of the younger artists who are trying to make art change the world, doing reclamation art projects in degraded sites, creating dialogue between polarized groups, working in foster homes. At the Battle of Seattle, it was exactly those groups that I met, who were behind the great sense of carnival, designing flags and puppets, dropping banners from impossible sites. I thought then, and I think now, that they are an energetic future for art that is helping to knit art and life back together again.

The great economist John Maynard Keynes talked about the hideous waste of an economic system that could not recognize art or beauty. In a speech to the Irish Government in 1933, he urged politicians and economists – because they had power – to raise their ambition, and spend the money on beauty: 'For what we have spent on the dole in England since the war', he complained, 'we could have made our cities the greatest works of man in the world.'

Keynes himself was an economist with a deep interest in art. He launched the Arts Council, poured money and investment into the Cambridge Arts Theatre and married a ballerina. We might take his word for this. Yet a short walk through the outer estates of many of the greatest cities in Europe, let alone America or Asia, betrays the hideous ugliness that we expect large groups of the world's population to live in. Often it is ugliness that has been deliberately designed as a concrete monstrosity, using regeneration money that remains an unpaid debt long after the new bastilles have crumbled away.

Nor is it just the buildings. It is the litter, pollution, and inhuman absence of green trees and plants, which are a vital human need. Why is it that our masters believe that the poor uniquely need nothing green or natural in their lives?

So as minister of public space, you can expect me to argue in the Cabinet that the ambition of beautification means a different kind of measure of success, a different currency and a different means. It is an objective that requires human ingenuity, human warmth and imagination. Nor is there a trade-off between beauty and economic success. The most successful places on the planet are mostly beautiful, and if they are not they don't remain successful for long. Because people want to live there and invest in places that make them feel alive.

I have spent a quarter of a century or more trying to use retailing as a lever to change the world, so I am not one of those puritans who thinks that shopping should be beneath the notice of civilized people. But beautifying our public space is not primarily about shopping: consumerism will not help us here. Retail-led regeneration will need beautifying in itself. What we will need is a new currency altogether: we will succeed or fail according to how much imagination is in circulation. We will succeed to the extent to which we encourage human connection and conversation. We will succeed also to the extent to which we spend the small change of imagination – the human stories about people and places and what they aspire to do.

Ann Pettifor

How to Afford the Things that Matter

We have to live in hovels, not because we cannot build palaces, but because we cannot 'afford' them. The same rule of self-destructive financial calculation governs every walk of life. We destroy the beauty of the countryside because the unappropriated splendours of nature have no economic value. We are capable of shutting off the sun and the stars because they do not pay a dividend. London is one of the richest cities in the history of civilization, but it cannot 'afford' the highest standards of achievement of which its own living citizens are capable, because they do not 'pay'.

If I had the power today, I would surely set out to endow our capital cities with all the appurtenances of art and civilization on the highest standards . . . convinced that what I could create I could afford . . . once we allow ourselves to be disobedient to the test of an accountant's profit, we have begun to change our civilization.

John Maynard Keynes, 'National Self-sufficiency', 1933

I have just returned from a trip to Africa with the World Health Organization (WHO), whose senior staff are concerned about maternal and child mortality on the continent. In Dar es Salaam I was told that the Government cannot afford the rubber gloves needed by midwives during childbirth, and so mothers have to purchase these before arriving to give birth. The Government – unwilling to be 'disobedient to the test of an IMF accountant's profit' – cannot afford to train and hire midwives, so in Dar's Temeke hospital there are only six trained midwives working three shifts a day. During each shift there could be three caesareans and one or two unexpected haemorrhages; at the same time about thirty-five to forty normal births take place. The Ministry of Health cannot afford to staff additional wards and beds so women lie in rows on the hard, cold stone floor, covered only in their cotton 'kangas'. Not surprising then that Tanzania has one of the highest maternal and child mortality rates.

From there I travelled to South Africa where 12 million black people are homeless. The Government cannot afford, it appears, the $49 billion needed to meet its target of 2.4 million homes by 2014. South Africa's banks agreed in 2004 to make 42 billion rand available for low-income homebuyers by 2008. However, less than half of that has been provided as the banks are wary of the risks posed by market forces and instead wait for the Government to underwrite part of their lending.

Soon after arriving back home, the Royal Society for the Protection of Birds' magazine dropped through the door, and lifted my spirits. British RSPB members are trying to save Sumatra's Harapan Rainforest for birdlife by protecting it from logging and other destructive commercial activities. Can £2 million be raised from RSPB enthusiasts like me to recapture the appropriated splendours of the Harapan forest? Or will the lack of that thing we call money mean that Harapan's splendours, its tigers, exotic birds, insects, trees and flora must fall prey to the loggers?

It seems so. For we live in a global economy that worships the god Money – a god, that like so many other fearsome and destructive gods remains mysterious, mesmerizing, mercurial and magical. And the more destructive the god of money, the more obeisant humanity seems to become as we genuflect daily at the temples erected to its worship – be they banks, credit cards, hedge funds or 'private equity'.

Can we wake up from this collective stupor? Can we challenge the magical powers of that out-of-control god? Can we learn to understand that its powers, like the powers of the broomstick in The Sorcerer's Apprentice, *are powers that we can control and regulate, if only we had the will? Can we once again subordinate money values to human and environmental values? Do good lives really have to cost the Earth?*

I think not; but only if we learn to control money and money-lenders – by understanding money and money-creation; and by grasping that it has virtues if created, regulated and lent in the interests of society and the ecosystem.

Most of us believe that banks have money – in the form of either cash or bank money, to lend to us when we need it to build a house, finance a maternity ward or save a rainforest. Many of us still assume – wrongly – that bank loans represent a gift from someone who, unlike ourselves, has taken the trouble to deny themselves a portion of their income, and then save it by depositing it in a piggy-bank or savings account. Part of our reverence for banks and bankers is rooted in this assumption.

We are not alone in holding to this delusion. Most mainstream economists still believe that banks have 'savings' – either theirs, or those of others – and extend these savings to others as credit – charging interest for the trouble they have taken.

This is not the case. *The money for a bank loan does not exist until we, the customers – whether we be individuals, or corporations or governments – apply for credit. Reserves are created to support lending.*

How, you ask, can this be? Let's begin at the beginning.

By law, a bank is obliged to offer cash to its customers according to *demand,* depending, of course, on their credit standing or overdraft limit. As a consequence banks have to hold a ratio of deposits in the bank, as *cash.* This is known as the *cash ratio* or 'reserve requirement'. This tends to be a small fraction of total deposits.

A popular illusion persists: that banks can only lend on the basis of reserve requirements. In other words, to lend £1,000, banks need a reserve requirement of £100 in their vaults.

The reality is exactly the opposite. In other words, far from the bank starting with a deposit, and then lending out money, the bank starts with our application for a loan, the asset against which we guarantee repayment, such as our house, and the promise we make to repay with interest. A clerk then enters the number into a ledger. Having agreed the loan, the commercial bank then applies to the central bank which provides – on demand – the necessary *cash* element of the loan.

This cash element (notes and coins) is the small proportion of the loan that will be *tangible* to the borrower. The rest is bank money, which is *intangible* – that is, you never touch, see or feel it. (Think of bank transfers; of mortgage payments; of internet banking.) Once the commercial bank has obtained the cash from the central bank we the borrowers then obligingly re-deposit both the *bank money* (the intangible, undrawn part of the loan) and the tangible cash, which together make up the sum of the loan, in either our own, or in other banks – *creating deposits.* Even if we spend the cash, the recipient of our cash will deposit it.

So it is our application for funds or for a loan, that creates deposits in banks, and that generates both cash and bank money.

Cash vs Bank Money

In the UK in 1982 the ratio of coins and notes to bank deposits was 1:14. At the end of 2005 the ratio had more than doubled, to 1:34. Put differently: in 1982 there was about £10.5 billion in circulation as *notes and coins*. Retail and wholesale deposits –

i.e. bank money – amounted to almost fourteen times as much: £144 billion. By 2005 there was only £38 billion circulating in notes and coins, and almost thirty-four times as much – £1,289 billion – held in banks as retail and wholesale deposits (Office for National Statistics, May 2006).

So for every £1 circulating in cash in 2005, £34 took the intangible form of bank money, or deposits. We call this intangible bank money, *free money.* Much is, quite literally, lent into existence, conjured from the digital banking ether in response to our desire to grow.

These historic numbers demonstrate that the ratio of cash to bank money is not a constant: cash declines over time as confidence in bank money grows, and we make ever-greater use of, for example, credit cards, bank transfers and internet banking.

The central bank of a country is the only authority with the power to issue notes and coins. The cash withdrawn by commercial banks from the central bank (say, the Bank of England) is only a small proportion of the total that the commercial bank loans out: £1 in cash for every £22 in bank money lent out. So if the commercial bank demands £300 from the Bank of England in cash, it is proposing to make a loan of £6,600.

The commercial bank pays a fee (generally known as interest) to the central bank on for example the £300 of cash drawn down for the loan outlined above. It pays no interest at all on the balance of *free bank money* – £6,300. The borrower however, will be paying an interest rate above the official rate of, say, 5 per cent – possibly 8 per cent – on the whole amount of £6,600.

The less cash there is in the economy, the more *free money* the banks create. This might illuminate the intention behind an advertising campaign run by the Maestro credit card company in the UK, in 2006/7.

'Cash is oh-so-last-millennium.'
'Cash stinks.'

'Money talks. Coins just make a racket.'
Maestro: 'the new cash'.

It gets worse. Not only do banks charge interest on this free money, which *we, the borrowers*, have created by applying for a loan – they add a range of unnecessary charges that in the UK brings in about £3 billion ($6 billion) a year in additional revenue. These include charges for overdrawing on authorized overdrafts; arrangement fees for loans; charges for 'premium' account holders (which ensure that telephone calls are answered!) etc.

Money is a Free Good

So how much can banks lend given that they do not need to find money/deposits in the first place? The answer is that there are no limits to the creation of bank money and therefore of credit, and like other free goods, the price (or interest) should be very low.

The cost to a bank or finance company of entering numbers into a ledger is ludicrously low, or non-existent. Note too, that the cost of obtaining cash from the central bank is passed on to the borrower. If pushed, bankers would explain that their costs for creating money in the form of a loan, involve an infinitesimally small share of the cost of the ledger, of the pen or computer; of the wage of the member of staff that enters the number; and of the rental costs of the building. With the development of technology, and with the growth of credit, these fixed costs disappear.

The modern banking system manufactures money out of nothing. The process is perhaps the most astounding piece of sleight-of-hand that was ever invented. Banking was conceived in inequity and born in sin . . . But if you want to continue to be slaves of the bankers and pay the cost of your own slavery, then let the bankers continue to create money and control credit.

> Josiah Charles Stamp (1880–1941), English economist,
> President of the Bank of England in the 1920s
> and the second richest man in Great Britain

Given these very low costs, and given that there is no limit to the volume of credit/debt that can be created, then credit is essentially *a free good*. Prices in free markets are supposed to rise for scarce resources. There is (as yet) for example, no price for the air we breathe, because there is no (apparent) limit to it; and it is not scarce. In the same way, there is no scarcity of credit; no limit to its creation.

There should therefore be no limit to the amount of money that can be created for the building of maternity wards and homes, for paying midwives and purchasing clinical gloves, and for saving the rainforest.

Keynes understood that money was essentially a free good. In his *Treatise on Money*, he wrote:

> Why then . . . if banks can create credit, should they refuse any reasonable request for it? And why should they charge a fee for what costs them little or nothing?
>
> Keynes, 1930.

The answer of course is that if the bank is a publicly-owned bank, a bank answerable to the citizens of a nation, then there is no reason why it should charge a fee, or interest, for what costs little or nothing. There is no reason why it should not create debt-free (i.e. non-interest bearing) money for public works. If publicly-owned banks, or the Government, exercised the power to create credit for public works, citizens would not have to raise funds for maternity wards, houses and the rain-forest by transferring part of their income to governments in the form of taxes (or donations to the RSPB!).

President Lincoln, Henry Ford and Thomas Alva Edison (the latter were both brilliant engineers) all argued for governments to exercise such powers. Ford and Edison made the case in an extended debate about the financing of a dam, in the *New York Times* in December, 1921. Ford wrote:

Army engineers say it will take $40,000,000 to complete that big dam [Muscle Shoals dam]. But Congress . . . is not in the mood to raise the money by taxation.The customary alternative is thirty-year bonds at 4 per cent. The United States, the greatest government in the world, wishing $40,000,000 to complete a great public benefit *is forced to go to the money sellers to buy its own money.* [My emphasis] At the end of thirty years the Government not only has to pay back the $40,000,000 but it has to pay 120 per cent interest, literally, has to pay $88,000,000 for the use of $40,000,000 for thirty years . . . Think of it. Could anything be more childish, more unbusinesslike?

Whenever the Government needs money for a great public improvement, instead of thinking of bonds with heavy interest charges, think of redeemable non-interest bearing currency . . . Do you appreciate that 80 cents of every dollar raised by taxation is spent in the payment of interest? . . . Here is a way to get the improvements without increasing the debt.

The interest load is breaking down our whole financial system. It is simply a case of thinking and calculating in terms different than those laid down to us by the inter-national banking group to which we have grown so accus-tomed that we think there is no other desirable standard. . . . The only difference between the currency plan and the bond plan is that there is no interest to be paid and the Wall Street money merchants, who do nothing to build the dam and deserve nothing, will get nothing. . . . The function of the money-seller will have disappeared.

Boyle, 2002

I leave to your imagination what ruses the money merchants used to ensure that Henry Ford's sensible advice was never taken by the US government.

During Henry Ford's time, governments exercised some regulatory controls over money merchants. Since the late 1970s, governments led by Presidents Richard Nixon and Ronald Reagan, and Mrs Thatcher, have removed more and more of the regulatory controls that governed the money merchants, and the creation of credit. Today the creation of money or credit, and its counterpart – debt – appears to be out of control, and is financing the growing wealth of those fortunate enough to own assets – including financial assets. These assets are distributed unevenly – midwives, the home-less and rainforests generally do not qualify – which in turn has led to the massive enrichment of the already-rich, and a growing gulf between rich and poor.

Like the Sorcerer's Apprentice, the 'broomstick' that is the international financial system is now beyond the reach of its masters – those deemed 'guardians of the nation's finances' – central bank governors and finance ministers. Instead the private, virtually unregulated finance sector has created a global 'credit bubble' (which is also a debt bubble) which has financed other bubbles (think of property/stocks and shares/vintage jewellery/works of art). This bubble has in turn led to extraordinary financial imbalances, and instability. Many, including this author, have warned that the global credit bubble is bound to burst; that its bursting will be devastating. And that all that is in question is the timing of the credit implosion.

Bank Money: the Democratization of Lending and Borrowing

Now while it is true that politicians, governments and the private banking sector have encouraged us to turn bank money into the equivalent of the out-of-control broomstick conjured up by the Sorcerer's Apprentice, we must not forget that bank money is a thing of great virtue.

The fundamental reasons for its virtue are twofold. The first is this: *Bank money is not the result of economic activity; bank money creates economic activity.*

To raise money in ancient times, borrowers would have had to try and save money over time, or would have had to approach a member of the local elite; a powerful landlord or warlord who had accumulated assets and savings (by, no doubt, brutal and dubious means). This member of the elite would have lent reluctantly; and at very high rates of interest.

The invention of bank money – money that did not depend on existing economic activity, but *created* economic activity – meant that borrowers could end their dependency on those who were already rich. Bank money provided a mechanism for lending that precisely did not depend on the generosity or meanness of individuals holding savings towards those who did not have savings.

As a result, bank money widened and democratized the allocation of credit. After the invention of bank money, to the astonishment and delight of many, money was no longer a scarce resource. *Once banks are able to create credit, investment is no longer constrained by saving.* (Chick 1983; Davidson 1986; Thirlwall 1999; and Studart 1995. All in Tily 2005).

Economic activity was no longer bound up with, and dependent on the already-rich. This was indeed a liberating and great social advance. However, for bank money to be sustainable, it had to be loaned at rates of interest compatible with human society's priorities; and with the limits of the ecosystem. For governments, the money, as Henry Ford argued, should be interest-free. For others, it had to be *cheap money*. Cheap money makes most economic activity possible. Cheap money makes it possible, for example, to research, design and build long term, whether it be the restoration of rainforests, the building of homes or the payment of midwives' salaries.

However, if bank money is placed under the control of the private finance sector, then money is allocated for the purpose of the private gain of 'money-sellers', not public benefit.

Keynes was aware of the great virtues of bank money; of how it could be used to end poverty; and of how short-sighted is the 'financial calculation' of the private sector. Those who argue we cannot *afford* well-paid, well-trained midwives; or money to house 12 million homeless South Africans; or the money needed to protect a rainforest.

Bank money and the power to set interest rates

Bank money has a second great advantage, the very thing that had motivated its invention: lower interest rates. Karl Marx was fully aware that bank money took place 'as a reaction against usury':

> The development of the credit system takes place as a reaction against usury. . . . this violent fight against usury . . . robs usurers' capital of its monopoly by concentrating all fallow money reserves and throwing them on the money-market. . . .

> Marx, 1894

The invention of bank money enabled the lowering of the rate of interest to sustainable levels. Instead, under a system of bank money, public banks could both increase the supply of money, and lower its price: the rate of interest. Which is why bank money, regulated properly, and in the hands of a publicly accountable institution, under proper constraints, can be a very good thing.

Those of us who live in the privileged and exploitative economies of the West can all play a part in bringing about a transformation to the international financial system. We can do it by increasing our understanding of the system. And we can do it by declining to dance to Finance's tune. After all, the finance sector depends on us, the world's debtor-spenders, to come to the ball. We can turn down the invitation. We can decline the credit card, overdraft or loan. We can live within our means.

We need not sit passively by, believing that our man-made structures are 'natural' or permanent. That financial powers are so entrenched that wrenching them away from the finance sector would require a revolution. Sure, there will be dogged resistance from those greatly enriched by current arrangements, we need to remind ourselves that in a crisis, the finance sector will be only too happy to transfer its losses and liabilities to the public sector; i.e. to you and me, hard-working taxpayers. Indeed it is already doing so, by transferring responsibility for private pension fund losses to taxpayers.

We need not give up because new technology means that 'the genie is out of the bottle', and cannot be put back again. Not so. We are not after all governed by a monster called technology. We govern technology. We must not assume that the power to create free money and issue endless credit, the ability to use this power to extract wealth from others, and make a claim on the future are powers that are irreversible and fixed in stone. They are not. The world really does not have to be this way. We can change it.

Larry Elliott

The Difference between Misery and Happiness . . .

Mr Micawber would consider us a sorry lot. We all know Mr M.'s famous dictum: 'Annual income twenty pounds, annual expenditure nineteen pounds nineteen and six, result happiness. Annual income twenty pounds, annual expenditure twenty pounds ought and six, result misery.'

Excellent philosophy. The problem is that fewer and fewer of us live by it. Bankruptcy no longer results – as it did in poor Micawber's case – in a sojourn to a debtors' prison, which is just as well for the Government, since the 100,000-plus people who went bust in 2006 would more than double at a stroke the number of people serving time at Her Majesty's pleasure.

But what it does illustrate is that Britain is a country that is living beyond its means at every level, personal, national and environmental. The idea of personal thrift has gone out of the window, to be replaced by a culture in which it is not just permissible but commonplace – acceptable even – to live beyond our means.

The justification for the borrowing is that most of it is secured against bricks and mortar, and the value of that asset has been rising rapidly. Yet, the shaky foundations for this economic model would be quickly exposed were house prices to start falling, particularly if that retrenchment were to be combined – as it was in the early 1990s – with rising unemployment. In those circumstances, the debt-financed model of consumption would be exposed for what it is: the dodgiest sort of leveraged buy-out: we borrow to the hilt to buy assets that are then used as their own collateral.

This excess of consumption is reflected at the next level – that of the balance of payments. It is now a quarter of a century since the UK last ran a surplus on manufactured goods, but for a while North Sea oil disguised the growing problem Britain was having in making ends meet. At its peak in the mid-1980s, oil was worth more than £8 billion a year to the balance of payments, but the wells are rapidly running dry. For the past decade, the size of the current account deficit has been getting steadily larger, despite a strong performance by the service sector and the best efforts of City speculators, who have made more money on their risky investments overseas than foreign investors have made on their safe but boring punts in the UK.

Something, as the ever-optimistic Mr Micawber predicted, may well turn up to alleviate the problem. It is conceivable, just, that a severe recession of the sort seen at the start of the 1990s would result in a backlash against the live-now, pay-later society, or that a pronounced fall in the value of the pound coupled with some austerity tax measures might push the trade figures back into the black. That is certainly what happened in the years running up to the arrival of Tony Blair in Downing Street. Big increases in taxation bore down on consumer spending, with resources diverted into investment and exports. But since 1996, the last year in which the UK ran a current account surplus, the old bad habits of the British economy have returned. Consumption has been in excess of production; house prices have doubled; a million or more jobs in manufacturing have been lost. Sooner or later the economy will arrive at reality checkpoint; the moment when the foreign investors who have been backing the pound decide to up sticks and move their cash elsewhere. It's happened before and it will almost certainly happen again.

The consequent recession will be painful and quite possibly protracted, but in the end Britain will get over it. In the long term, life will go on.

The same, sadly, could not be said of the environment, where Britain and the rest of the developed world are sleep-walking towards climate change Armageddon. Think 1962 and the Cuban missile crisis; it's of that order of magnitude. Decisions that will be taken over the next five to ten years are going to have a profound impact on the future of the planet. When it comes to the environment, it is not just a question of cutting our coat according to our cloth for a few years and then returning to business as usual. Why? Because business as usual – living beyond our ecological means and, by example, encouraging the developing world to do the same – is a death knell for the planet.

Policy-makers have only just started to wake up to the enormity of the challenge. They have started to make serious speeches about climate change, which is progress of a sort. Tony Blair commissioned a heavyweight economist, Sir Nicholas Stern, to prepare a weighty tome on the economics of climate change. At the 2007 G8 summit, Western leaders committed themselves to a strategy that would mean a 50 per cent cut in greenhouse gas emissions by 2050. It all sounded mightily impressive. It sounded as if the G8 – even George Bush – was finally getting it. The problem, however, is that while policy-makers talk like John F. Kennedy they act like Viv Nicholson.

For those who can't remember back that far, Ms Nicholson won a small fortune on the pools in 1961 – a year when the first wave of the post-war consumer society was in full swing. She was a blonde for whom the clichés 'bubbly' and 'blowsy' seemed for once appropriate, for when she picked up her big cheque in London she announced amid a sea of flashbulbs that she had no intention of going back to her old life – trying to make ends meet on £7 a week in Castleford – but was going to party hard.

When newspapers trot out the ritual 'spend, spend, spend' headline they are paying homage to Ms Nicholson's commitment to blow the lot – a pledge she duly fulfilled. She became an iconic figure. There was a play of her life and she appeared on the cover of a single by the band The Smiths. But when it comes to live now, pay later, she was an amateur compared with today's hedonists.

A Mintel survey showed that in 2006 consumer spending broke through the £1 trillion barrier – 9 per cent up on the previous year. Foreign holidays, champagne, glossy magazines chronicling the lifestyles of celebrities: all have now, apparently, become integral parts of the good life. Things have moved on since Harold Macmillan announced fifty years ago that Britain had 'never had it so good'. Then, the family that wanted to live it up aspired to bundling the kids into an Austin 7 for two weeks in Blackpool or Margate; now couples at a loose end as the weekend approaches think about a weekend break in Prague or Vilnius. In the autumn of 2006, shortly after the launch of the Stern review, the newspapers were full of stories about British consumers taking advantage of the cheap pound and cut-price fares to do their Christmas shopping in Manhattan.

Governments have encouraged policies that threaten to cost the earth. However concerned they may be that global temperatures may be a couple of degrees higher by the middle of the century, they are far more concerned about being returned at the next general election. And policies that make flying or driving more expensive could cost votes.

There are, despite the abundance of scientific evidence, still some people who believe that the threat from climate change has been exaggerated. But let's assume that they are wrong and that the precautionary principle militates a crash rethink of the way in which we live our lives. Is any such reappraisal under way? Sadly not.

Macmillan's famous phrase was mentioned by Mervyn King in the spring of 2007, although the governor of the Bank of England put the words into their proper context, namely a warning by the then prime minister that he had his doubts about whether the good times could continue if policy-makers failed to deal with the threat of rising inflation. We now need to ask whether the good times can continue if policy-makers fail to deal with the threat of rising sea levels. The simple answer is that they cannot.

King and his fellow members of the monetary policy committee certainly believe that things have got a bit out of hand on the spending front in recent years. After the 9/11 attacks, central banks were concerned that the global economy would seize up. So they flooded the financial system with plenty of easy money, unleashing a wave of speculation that not only pushed up asset prices but threatened to spill over into inflation. Carbon emissions rose as well, but it was the threat to price stability that prompted the Bank of England, the Federal Reserve and the European Central Bank to nudge up interest rates.

King expressed his unease about the economy's over-reliance on consumption, noting that the current account deficit was worryingly large and that there needed to be a rebalancing of the economy so that investment and exports were substituted for consumer spending.

This will be easier said than done. Back in 1957, the big picture of the economy looked similar to that of 2007 – steady growth for a prolonged period, inflation between 2 and 3 per cent, low unemployment (lower than today, in fact) coupled with concerns about Britain's competitiveness and ability to pay its way in the world. Macmillan's Government, though, had more weapons at its disposal; consumer demand was regulated through credit controls; there were import curbs to help boost exports; and there was stricter property taxation to keep house prices in check. One feature of the so-called Golden Age was that – until the last couple of years before the 1973 Yom Kippur war – there was nothing remotely resembling a property boom.

Today, the main instrument for regulating the economy is the bank rate, supported to some extent by Gordon Brown's fiscal rules. That can make life difficult for policy-makers, since it is almost impossible to set borrowing costs at a level that will keep consumer spending buoyant enough to maintain a growth level consistent with hitting the inflation target. What tends to happen is that rates are, for a time, reduced to a level that sets off wild speculation in the housing market. When people are borrowed up to the eyeballs and house prices are soaring, rates are pushed up to a level that causes enough pain for borrowing, spending growth and house prices to moderate. If the distress becomes too acute, rates are cut and the cycle starts again.

We are at the point where some analysts want the Bank to bang up rates to at least 6 per cent and others warn of the risks of overkill. Either way, any period of belt-tightening will be temporary, when what is needed – both for the economy and, more crucially, for the planet – is a prolonged period of restraint, moderation and thrift.

No question, consumers are more alive to the risks of global warming than they were ten or even five years ago. That's true of other countries as well; indeed, countries like Germany are streets ahead of Britain when it comes to investing in renewable energy.

The debate over climate change makes a revolution in attitudes less difficult than it might appear, but only marginally. It is good news that the Government has finally woken up to the risks of global warming; less encouraging that it persists in the fantasy that cutting emissions is consistent with a business-as-usual, go-for-growth economic strategy.

New Labour has always been a political movement that has wanted to have its cake and eat it, and nowhere is this more true than over climate change. Both the then prime minister Tony Blair and his successor Gordon Brown turned up to the launch of the Stern review, as if to emphasize that concern about the environment went right to the top of Government. Yet within a month, the Government was endorsing two reports – the Barker review of planning and the Eddington review of transport – that proposed concreting over large chunks of the green belt and expanding the capacity of Britain's airports. The Government's message was that it was possible to be green while at the same time maximizing economic growth.

- Ministers would be better off if they levelled with us. The foundation stone of the new frugality is to admit to ourselves that we can continue to breeze off to Riga for the weekend courtesy of Michael O'Leary or take action to stop temperatures rising. We can't do both.
- A second necessity is for a reappraisal of what constitutes the good life. Economic success is judged by what happens to Gross Domestic Product (GDP). If GDP goes up by 4 per cent that is twice as good as it going up by 2 per cent, but not quite as good as if it went up by 5 per cent. In a country where the population is living on the edge of starvation this crude measure has relevance; in the Britain of 2007 it does not. The measure of domestic progress published by the New Economics Foundation is just one piece of work showing that the link between economic growth and well-being is tenuous once a modest level of prosperity is reached. That, though, is not the way the economic system works. It operates on the basis that there is no such thing as enough.

- Third, the Government has to be more serious about incentives for households to go green. The pitiful amount allocated for grants to install renewable energy into the home is one example of a lack of real commitment; ministers should be providing tax breaks for households to generate their own energy and insulate homes. Britain has a small but innovative environmental industry sector; far more could be done by stimulating demand for anti-pollution technologies at home and work.

Given that the spend, spend, spend culture is closely linked to the excesses of the property market, a fourth feature of any new regime would be more stringent taxes to prevent house-price inflation. Various methods have been proposed, including capital gains tax on prime residences, a Danish-style annual property tax that rises in line with house prices and a tax on land values. All have their merits and their adherents. All are seen as politically unacceptable.

But unless we are prepared to show more restraint, there is not the slightest possibility of India and China signing up to a new binding global treaty to tackle climate, and the idea of 2.5 billion people following Ms Nicholson's example doesn't really bear thinking about.

4

Good Food

Following the principle that some of the best meals are simple, contain just a handful of good quality, well-prepared ingredients and are light enough not to leave you groaning, **Hugh Fearnley-Whittingstall**, founder of The River Cottage serves up an hors-d'oeuvre on the importance of local food, but also why we shouldn't be absolutist about such things. Food is the area, he tells us, in which it is easiest to go green. But watch out, he says, as soon as you start trying to do the right thing, people expect you to be perfect and call you a hypocrite if you fail to live up to their expectations. We should relax, Hugh argues. If you do nothing else, try to buy local. That will mean your food is also seasonal and therefore is likely to have the least environmental impact.

Our main course is prepared by the *éminence grise* of green food and farming, **Colin Tudge**. A regular contributor to *New Scientist* magazine for many years, and author of several books, including *So Shall We Reap* and *Feeding People is Easy*, Colin has prepared a radical dish of ideas about how to change the food chain. To feed a growing world population and still live within our environmental limits, Colin says we will need to ditch our obsession with a global market in food built on beggar-thy-neighbour competition, and learn from nature how to cooperate more. There are two main ingredients. First, he argues that corporate power needs to be finely chopped down to size. Without this, there is little hope that we can design a food system likely to be able to feed the people who need it most. Second, we need to bust the myth

that wanting good quality food that has not been hom-
ogenized and shrink-wrapped by supermarkets is a middle
class fantasy. This is merely ignorance, argues Colin, because
all the great cuisines in the world, including French and
Italian, are based on peasant cooking. Simple ingredients, well
cooked. To promote an alternative, he suggests a 'network of
networks' of the best approaches and calls for a World Wide
Food Club, backed by a College for Enlightened Agriculture,
to make it happen.

For dessert, complete with after dinner conversation, we
have a dish from **Rosie Boycott,** one of Britain's leading
commentators and author of *Our Farm*. She mixes an eclectic
range of ingredients together, including a Victorian bathing-
wagon, cheap flights to Australia and a smallholding. You will
find reflections on the hardships and pleasures of small island
life, and a deep questioning of the real character of progress.
Rosie reminds us of something that is easy to forget in our
high-tech, service-driven economy in which virtual reality
appears increasingly to displace the real world. All life
depends on plants. You may love wi-fi, 'second life' and the
limitless potential of digital entertainment, but if plant leaves
stop photosynthesizing, or bees stop pollinating, you're dead.
Our lack of respect for nature and reckless waste and over-
consumption are driving climate change. But it doesn't have
to be this way. Discuss, late into the night. . . .

Hugh Fearnley-Whittingstall

How Green is your Orange?*

It is, of course, marvellous being green. Recycle your bottles, re-use your shopping bags, compost your waste, insulate your loft and get yourself a bicycle. Then swagger about, feeling like you're saving the planet, without the indignity of having to dive into a phone box and put your knickers on outside your trousers. Or so it seems at first.

But if, like me, you've been trying to be green for some years, the sheer relativity of it all (as in, 'well, it's all relative, isn't it') can start to get you down. I hear they're calling it Green Fatigue.

Take oranges, for example. We get through a lot of them in our house and we always choose fairly traded, organic fruit. This, I believe, is a positive green/ethical choice. Yes, there are food miles – but I can't grow oranges at home, not even in my polytunnel. And somewhere, in north Africa or South America, is a farmer who not only is spared the risk of spraying dangerous pollutant chemicals on his orange trees without the proper safety equipment, but who also gets a decent price for his fruit.

And all because we, and others, choose it to go into our electric citrus juicers every morning. Our oranges are so green they practically give us haloes. But what do we do with the squeezed-out orange shells? Usually, our kitchen trimmings get composted or fed to the chickens. But chickens don't like orange peel, and it won't break down in the compost heap either. So I find myself throwing those orange shells in the dustbin and feeling really bad about it. (Well, quite bad. There is a feeble hesitation before each empty half-orange is lobbed. But the bin is at the opposite side of the kitchen from the juicer, and the negative vibes are increasingly outweighed by the satisfaction of a direct hit.)

Recently I've been told you can compost citrus fruit but that they require their own private bin, in which to develop a luscious thick jumper of fluffy green mould, before they can join the rest of the vegetation and rot down in an obliging manner. This option is under review, and will be voted on in the next session of FHERC (pronounced fur-herk, that's the Fearnley Household Environmental Review Council). As it happens, there are currently no plans to convene the council. In other words, we're not sure we can really be arsed on this one.

I mean, FHERC's sake! I've always tried to be honest about the imperfect nature of my ethical journey ('Of course, it's impossible not to be a hypocrite' is practically my catchphrase). Nevertheless, I deeply resent having the imperfections and contradictions of my attempts at green living pointed out to me by a third party. You know the kind of person – some smug cleverclogs who delights in revealing to you the misguided nature of your choices.

'There's no point in recycling glass!' he'll tell you, then wait for you to ask why not. You will of course oblige. And he will say, 'Because the silica from which glass is made is effectively an unlimited resource. I mean, it's just sand. At the current rate of consumption, the world would not run out of sand for 12 billion years. Recycling a bottle uses eleven times more energy than processing raw silicon, and that doesn't include the petrol you use to drive to the bottle bank. . . .' At this point I am wondering if it would be a waste of energy to smack the speaker in the mouth.

To make it easy on yourself, and avoid the constant torment of FECS (Flawed Environmental Conscience Syndrome), you should know (or at least believe, as I do) that food is the area in which it's easiest and most pleasurable to go green, and get unambiguously planet-saving results.

It's easy because the tactics you need to embrace can be summarized in a two-word nutshell: 'buy local'. This for me is the ethical practice with the most unequivocal feel-good factor. Buy local food and, almost by definition, you're buying seasonal produce with a low environmental impact.

It's more pleasurable, because you will end up cooking and eating food that's produced with care and which, because it isn't cynically and scientifically designed, harvested and packed to survive long journeys, can be grown for flavour and quality. Finally, you can enjoy strawberries, for example, that taste as if they were grown to be eaten – not for surviving inter-galactic time warps.

Talking of which . . . it may or may not be possible for the collective actions of the environmentally concerned citizens of the world to save our planet. It may or may not already be too late. But by God it would make me miserable not to give it my best shot. I truly believe that, when it comes to trying to be green, even when you get it wrong, it's still the right thing to do.

I mean, what else are we going to do? Start rooting for the bad guy?

*A version of this article first appeared in *The Guardian*, 23 September 2006.

Colin Tudge

How the World Could Be, and How to Get There . . .

More and more people I speak to – respectable, middle class, middle-aged, middle of the road people – agree that the world can't go on as it is. If we go on as we are, we will have had our collective chips by the end of the twenty-first century. A fair slice of humanity has hit the buffers already (although most of them are in distant countries of which we prefer to know little). We, collective humanity, need to take stock, count our genuine assets – decide what goods, techniques, and ways of life are really worth hanging on to – and then start again from scratch, building upon whatever is worth rescuing from the present mess.

Some people don't agree with this, of course. They believe that humanity is on course, even if they cannot quite define what that course is supposed to be. Or, what it would be, were it not for the inconvenience of 'terrorists' and other troublemakers. Unfortunately, these are the people with most power; and who are doing very well out of the status quo. Chief among them are the big banks and corporations. Then there are elected governments such as those of George W. Bush and New Labour who depend upon the same corporations. Then come the intellectuals and experts who advise the financiers and policy-makers – economists, scientists, lawyers, accountants, and that new cadre of professional managers known as MBAs.

Of course, not all financiers, politicians, intellectuals and experts believe that the world is on course for better things, and support the status quo. But the objectors are generally

marginalized and find it harder to gain support for their
research than those who are onside. A few have apparent
kudos and positions of power – some have titles and director-
ships – but none commands the heights. It is hard to think of
anybody who is nice, and sensible, and has real power.

But what does it mean, to 'start again'? We must begin, I
suggest, by rethinking everything. What kind of creatures are
we? What manner of species? What do we need to stay alive?
What do we want? Are we basically nice, or basically nasty?
Are we capable of cooperation? Can we trust each other? Or
should we – as is now the standard recommendation – simply
compete, head to head, solipsistically from cradle to grave?

Is it good to have a vision at all, or is this presumptuous? If
we do define some future goals, by what means should we
achieve them? What kind of economy could translate our
needs and just desires into action? What kind of technologies?

Of course, it is important to question at every turn. Unless
we do so, the answers we come up with will not be robust.
And no answer is ever beyond further argument. Like moral
philosophers, we might ask at the outset, for example, 'And
who, pray, is "we" in this context?'

Such musing should, I suggest, be at the core of all education: everyone on this Earth asking, as a matter of course,
what it is right to do, and why.

But on the whole the things that matter most, the ideas that
are needed to hold humanity together, are left to hazard.
Moral thinking is not mainstream in modern society – or at
least, it is only ad hoc, as in the agony columns, as in, 'Should I
tell my boyfriend I have been unfaithful?' The deep principles
of morality (and indeed whether there are deep principles)
are not spelled out, except in formal philosophical texts which
for the most part are unreadable and in which, for the most
part, philosophers reveal that they have no more to say about
the condition of humanity than you might hear expatiated in

any saloon bar. (Moral philosophers, I have found, rarely translate their deep cogitations into recommendations that are of any practical use.)

But we cannot wait for the thinking through to be completed before we act. So here is my personal set of notions and principles, up for grabs.

Notions and Principles

Morality, I suggest, is about unselfishness: the conscious desire to benefit others, even at personal cost. Of course it can be risky. The person who is benefited might spit in your eye. But the risk is worth it. This is not an original thought. Jesus Christ was among the more prominent of those who expressed this view in the past.

I reject utilitarian ethics, summarized as 'the greatest happiness of the greatest number' – or at least, it is only of limited use. It depends, after all, on who is made happy, and what makes them happy. Nazis are happy when they beat up gypsies, but this cannot be good, even if the Nazis are in the majority. But neither is it easy to be absolutist – to try to define in absolute terms what a good action is. I am happiest with virtue ethics – which to me were most satisfactorily defined by the Hindu mystic Ramakrishna. The three fundamental attitudes to cling to, he said, are personal humility; respect for other, sentient creatures; and a sense of reverence.

Ramakrishna would have said, reverence for God. Pagans, or atheists, might prefer to think of reverence for the universe as a whole. Either way it is necessary to bear in mind that the universe is not of our making, and is not in our gift. Take these three tenets seriously and a huge amount of the nonsense that now dominates the airways and soaks up so much taxpayers' money would go to the wall. Everything from human cloning to the grand, vile, and irredeemably foolish notion that we can or should strive to 'conquer' nature is so obviously beyond all countenance, once we apply the most basic moral thinking.

Cooperation versus Competition

I also like the idea of humanity and of common cause – that we are all one, and all in it together. Tennyson opined in the 1830s that nature is 'red in tooth and claw'. In *Origin of Species*, written a generation later, Darwin seems to continue in that same vein. He speaks even in his subtitle of 'the preservation of favoured races' and 'the struggle for life'. Later, Herbert Spencer summarized *Origin of Species* as 'the survival of the fittest' – a phrase that Darwin then adopted. Darwin was a kind man, a good liberal who, for example, stood up to slave-owners on their own turf, in South America. He was also very aware that creatures cooperate in nature, and discussed co-evolution at length. But competition emerges from his writings as the prime driving force of nature and so it is still perceived, as if this were self-evident. I have heard modern tycoons – notably, one of the directors of Enron – claim that their ruthlessness is fine because it is 'natural'; a truly sublime concatenation of moral solecisms. Cooperativeness, unselfishness, altruism, are seen as eddies in the grand tide of general viciousness; and there is maths out there, in the form of game theory, to prove that this must be so.

In reality, of course, nature as a whole is at least as cooperative as it is competitive. Were it not so, there could be no biosphere at all – and indeed no universe. Even if it were not so, it has long been argued (from St Paul via David Hume to G.E. Moore and many others) that what is natural is not necessarily right. But in fact, it is just as natural to be social and cooperative as to be otherwise. Our innate psychology reflects the pattern of nature as a whole – as indeed it must since, as Darwin himself pointed out, our psychology has evolved like everything else about us. In short, biological theory, properly thought through, suggests not that human beings are likely to be nasty deep down, forever trying to get one up on each other, but are far more likely to be nice. Human beings can trust each other. Most of the time the people you help do not spit in your eye. The idea that we are basically nasty, and would be at each other's throats if not held in check, is a confidence trick perpetuated by people who want to be in charge, and to boss the rest of us about. Our deepest psychological flaw, I suggest, springs from our primate origins: far too great a respect for authority figures – alpha males who nowadays are in city clothes. We need to be able, like the little boy in Hans Christian Andersen's tale, to remind emperors that they have no clothes.

If people cooperate then the result, truly, can be win-win. Just to borrow a little utilitarian thinking for an instant, game theory also shows that we do achieve the greatest happiness of the greatest number when all pull together. No one individual in a truly cooperative society can be as rich as Croesus. Unlimited wealth is *verboten*. But everyone can do well. If we set out to create societies in which wealth is unlimited, then in the immediate term some will be very rich while the rest are poorer than they could otherwise be; and if everyone strives for maximum wealth, then society loses its conviviality, and indeed becomes vicious, and before long outstrips its resources and collapses. Exactly as is happening now.

Comfort levels

There are 6.5 billion people in the world now, and the projections suggest there will be 9 billion by 2050, remaining constant for the next 500 years or so. What kind of level could each individual expect to live at if all lived within a reasonable comfort zone – none abject and none as rich as Croesus and still rising? It is easy enough to work out. A consumption of energy worldwide roughly equivalent to what British people enjoyed in the 1950s should be possible and sustainable, with renewable energy. I was at school in the 1950s and life wasn't bad. We were cold now and again, but so what. Food was not as various as it seems to be these days but what there was, was very good (considering we were still recovering from the Second World War). My family had no car but it didn't seem to matter very much. Life was OK. One of the most OK things (though I took it for granted at the time) was that there was plenty for people to do.

Automation was of course well in train but most industries were still craft-based. Apprenticeship into some ancient and respected trade was still the norm. People left full-time education at anything between fifteen and thirty knowing that they had something useful to do for the rest of their lives – that they didn't have to work in a call centre, or serve burgers, or pay back student loans, or 'retrain' every five years but could just potter along with families and friends taking a pride during working hours in something they were practised in and did well. This in broad crude terms is the kind of material level that everyone could reasonably aspire to.

But, even within the material limits of the past, we can vastly improve on the past. Above all, I suggest, far and away the most pressing requirement in this crowded and beleaguered world, is to get the food supply right.

I argue in *So Shall We Reap* and *Feeding People is Easy* that for all kinds of reasons all nations (if we continue to suppose that 'nation' is a sensible unit) should strive to be self-reliant in food. This does not mean 'self-sufficient'. Self-sufficient means growing absolutely everything you might want which for most countries is not sensible. Britain, for instance, should not be trying to grow bananas or pineapples or ginger. Self-reliant means growing enough to get by. Then trade with other countries can be relaxed: each country can sell what it grows best and is able to grow in surplus, and each can buy in what it feels it needs to make life agreeable. Ideally trade would be restricted to foods that are low in volume and high in value – but we needn't be too puritanical about this.

Pineapples and bananas in big ships cooled by the sea itself (and perhaps wind-powered) seem perfectly reasonable. But countries that *rely* on exports or imports of food just to stay afloat – or, indeed, just to keep their people alive – are in hock to other countries and are particularly vulnerable now, when the climate is changing, and all output will become uncertain. In practice, the poor countries are in hock to the rich – and the rich make very sure that it stays that way, because their own economies depend on other people's relative poverty.

We live very well on our history. Britain would now be desperate indeed without cheap labour from countries poorer than ours: countries that once formed our own empire or were on the wrong side of the Cold War. But if poor countries at least are self-reliant in food – as most of them could be, in some cases several times over – then at least in theory they could keep the rich at bay. At least they would have the freedom to make their own mistakes. As things stand, world farming is totally dedicated to trade because trade is profitable to a minority, but no one is secure.

Long term security and self-reliance can be achieved only with agriculture that is subtle, and designed specifically to produce good food, humanely and without wrecking landscapes and traditional societies. Farming that is designed to feed people, as opposed to maximizing cash, I call 'Enlightened Agriculture'. Enlightened Agriculture is complicated – primarily it depends upon small, mixed farms with limited inputs of fossil fuels and industrial chemistry, and so it needs plenty of hands-on experts: farmers, in short. So agriculture designed to feed people, and to create self-reliance, must be labour-intensive. So all countries that aspire to self-reliance now and in the long term need a firm agrarian base.

Of course this can be overdone. In Rwanda, at present, 90 per cent of people work on the land, which the Rwandans themselves agree is too many. There aren't enough people left for the farmers to sell their produce to. On the other hand, the 1 per cent agrarian force that we now have in Britain and the United States, is ludicrously few. There are more people in gaol in the US than are full-time on the land.

The world needs a debate – the same debate that Adam Smith was having in the eighteenth century: what is the ideal proportion of people in town and country? To start the ball rolling, I would suggest on common sense grounds that no country should ideally have more than about 50 per cent of people on the land, and none should have fewer than about 20 per cent. This means that India, with around 60 per cent on the land, is roughly on course (which, I have found, many Indians agree with) while Britain and the US are seriously off-beam: out on a precarious limb. But the mantra has it that the fewer farmers, the better. Agrarian life is taken as a sign of backwardness (just as used to be true of forests). It's easy to forget that civilization once meant forest clearance – and in some countries still does.

Of course, agrarian living is difficult. Often it has been harsh. Zealots for urbanization use this as an excuse for throwing people off the land. They believe people are much better off in shanty towns where 1 billion people already live. But it depends how you tell the story. Agrarian societies have at times been the most agreeable in the world. You may not believe Tolstoy on this because he was an aristocrat, who could stop work when he chose. But we can believe John Clare, who had direct experience.

Farming can be an excellent job; none better. What makes it horrible is the long list of all that goes with it today: the very low kudos, resulting from very low income; the increasing isolation, because farmers are growing fewer on the ground; the lack of cultural opportunity, because of depopulation and because so little is invested in the countryside worldwide; the strain of bureaucracy; the dependence on the whim of super-markets, which are the chief buyers, with their constant pres-sure to reduce prices by whatever means; the reduction of the job from an exercise in husbandry and pastoral care to one of following the seed company's instructions – 'farming by numbers', as the expression has it.

The task before us, though, is to make agrarian living toler-able – and positively agreeable and desirable. Humanity needs plenty of good farmers if we are to be secure, and if the land-scape is to continue to be beautiful. We need to make it poss-ible, therefore, for people to farm – and a high proportion of people at that. The proper base for Enlightened Agriculture is what I call 'the New Agrarianism'.

So, what technologies can bring this about? Should we think high-tech, or low-tech? Does the future lie with genetic engineering or with smoother ox-carts?

The general answer was expressed by the Viennese philoso-pher Ivan Illich in the 1960s. He spoke of 'tools for conviviality'. He placed enormous store by the concept of autonomy: individ-uals and societies, he said, should above all control their own destiny. I like the term 'fulfilment'. Human well-being implies a basic degree of material comfort – good food, clean water, shelter, and confidence that your children will survive childhood.

After that, fulfilment is up to the individual to decide. Everything is fine (I would say) provided the means to fulfil-ment do not spoil other people's lives. But there is a bonus:

because most people are basically nice, and sensible, and cooperative, most people would achieve more fulfilment by cooperating than by battling and doing their neighbours down. Tools – technologies – that are anti-convivial are those that increase the power of minorities over the majority.

Illich identified the bicycle and the telephone as prime tools of conviviality. Both enable individuals to do their own thing in their own time; to go where they want, and to talk to whom they want. Both can be built and maintained on the small scale, enabling even small societies to be self-reliant. In principle at least, no one should need to buy a bike or a phone from some foreign-based multi-national. Neither technology is innately offensive. Bicycles do not wreck the landscape.

Modern science has hugely advanced the potential and range of convivial technologies. Bicycles are still with us – one of the great, fundamental technologies of all times, like sails, or the wheel itself. The telephone has grown conceptually speaking into the internet – a truly fabulous, and fabulously convivial technology. Indeed I see the net and all that goes with it – search engines, podcasts – as an evolutionary step for human beings. Human beings have become the dominant species not because we are individually clever – put most of us in a forest and I would not back our individual ingenuity against a hyena's – but because we can share our thoughts.

With the internet this huge potential for communication is given its head. You can grow pigeon peas at the edge of the desert and listen live to the Berlin Philharmonic. The greatest perceived disadvantage of rural life – living a backwater life – is removed at a stroke. The net is cheap. It can be run on solar power. Solar cells are among the most convivial of convivial technologies.

So the material basis of a future life that is convivial, in which people can be fulfilled, and which could last for ever – improving over time – is easy enough to envisage.

Agrarianism is not necessarily the norm, but it must again be the base, in all societies. The village again would emerge as the fundamental social unit. But people should flow freely from town to country depending on temperament, and at different times of their lives. I have seen a house in a Chinese village that would serve as a model for most of future humanity. It had pigs and poultry on the ground floor, as is traditional, and wall-to-wall electronics upstairs where the people lived. If the electronics was solar-powered we would have the basis of a complete lifestyle: sociality; intellectual stimulation; craft.

What kind of economy could support such a way of life? I used to favour Mao Zedong. Bad things happened in his regime and some of them continue to this day. Notably the gratuitous oppression of Tibet. But excellent things happened, too, including a peasant-based, very mixed, and complex agriculture which, for a time, here and there, was as good as agriculture gets; and for a time, too, here and there, real sociality prevailed. But as Mikhail Gorbachev said as the USSR broke up, centralized economies require people to behave in ways that do not come easily to them. They are too demanding. They also become bureaucratized and oppressive. For good measure, as many a western capitalist has pointed out, they are inefficient. Efficiency isn't the be-all and end-all. But it is good to be able to get something done without referring every decision to some committee.

So now I have come round again to capitalism – but emphatically not in current form, which is a horrible diversion. Adam Smith first extolled the free market in the eighteenth century; suggesting that an 'invisible hand' would ensure that society turned out well if everyone simply sold what they had to sell, and bought what they wanted, without worrying too much about creating any particular kind of society.

But Smith added two conditions, which some have chosen to forget. He was a moral philosopher before he was an economist. He felt that human beings were morally constrained by 'natural sympathy'. In other words, he knew that, for example, in any one village, three or four pubs might vie for trade. But no individual publican had any desire to be the only pub in town, or the only one in the land, at the expense of all the others. To Smith, the free market was as cooperative as it was competitive. Not nowadays. The Red Lion is not doing a good job until and unless it wipes the White Hart from the map.

Secondly, Smith knew that for the invisible hand to work, the market had to be 'ideal': an infinite number of traders and an infinite number of buyers, all with complete information and total freedom of choice. Anything less, and the market will succumb to special interests. Above all, Smith feared the corporates, and witnessed the East India Company, which became a law unto itself. He declared corporates to be the enemies of the free market.

Thomas Jefferson and his colleagues continued in this vein as they founded the United States. They wanted personal freedom for all and justice for all – but recognized that these two are to a significant extent in opposition. Indeed the US became the US when it did partly because of the excesses of the East India Company, which prompted the Boston Tea Party of 1773 which led in short order to the Declaration of Independence of 1776. So Jefferson framed laws to restrain the power of the corporates.

But in the late nineteenth century the corporates broke their Jeffersonian bonds. Now, they present themselves as the guardians of the free market, but in truth are its enemies. The task of corporates is not to make specific things, as traditional companies do. Their task and raison d'être is simply to generate as much wealth as possible, for their owners or shareholders.

It may be that corporates are good for some things. Clearly the wealth they generate is sometimes put to good use. They can if they choose build new schools or sports stadiums out of petty cash. This can be very seductive: an instant fix. But it is clear that corporate control is absolutely disastrous for the thing we most need to get right, which is food production. If we are to produce food for everyone, and for ever, then we have to respect biological limits. This means above all that we need to limit livestock production, and to fit livestock into the environments that they can genuinely enhance.

Basically this means sheep and cattle on grass where other crops cannot be grown, while pigs and poultry feed on left-overs and surpluses (as is common sense and is traditional). The total output of livestock must always be modest. 'Plenty of plants, not much meat, and maximum variety' summarizes all of modern nutritional theory in nine words.

As a very considerable bonus, plenty of plants, not much meat, and maximum variety is also the basis of all the greatest gastronomy. So enlightened agriculture – sensible farming within biological limits – does not lead us to austerity. Indeed, 'the future belongs to the gourmet'. But corporates must maximize wealth which means they need to maximize livestock production – for all kinds of reasons of which 'consumer preference' is low on the list. That is the route to disaster on all fronts.

Then again, agriculture that can truly serve the needs of humanity, for ever, also needs to be relatively labour-intensive. But to maximize profit, costs must be cut which means, perversely, reducing labour. This means farming must be simplified – complex sustainable systems go out of the window – and become monocultural, with all the dangers that that implies.

As labour-intensive farming gives way to monocultural industrial farming, too, millions upon millions of farmers are thrown out of work. Zealots for the status quo speak of 'alternative industries', but in truth there is no feasible alternative for the 2 billion or so people worldwide who now live on the land. Most will join their relatives and former workmates in the slums, until they die, which many do quite quickly. To sustain the status quo, energy is burnt and forests are felled, exacerbating global warming. Fresh water is squandered – perhaps the greatest folly of all. Landscapes are wrecked. Yet even so, a billion people are chronically undernourished. A billion more are dying before their time from the dreary catalogue of obesity, heart disease, diabetes, and diet-related cancers. The simplest statistics show that one-third of humanity is very badly served. But food corporates are constitutionally unable to do what the world requires.

So, I have become a capitalist; but absolutely not a corporate capitalist. We need to pick up the threads where Adam Smith and Thomas Jefferson left off. There are already some very promising economic models out there, not least developed by nef. These need to become the norm.

Indeed, all the required solutions are already out there. We have the moralities, and all the technologies we need, though with endless capacity to develop more. We have first-hand knowledge of economic systems that clearly do not work, and new models that promise improvement.

The future is networked

The remaining problem is the biggest – that of governance. The people who get to be in charge are the people who like power, and the people who like power are not necessarily on the side of humanity. To be glib, most people are nice but nasty people are on top.

For this reason, there simply is no point in being reformist, by asking governments and corporates to change their ways.

Neither will do more than is absolutely necessary to keep themselves in power, and all will dig their heels in as soon as they realize that their status is threatened. But, revolution is not advisable either. You never know how revolutions will turn out – babies tend to be thrown out with the bathwater. Besides, you'll lose. The law has been adjusted so that any of us could end up in Guantanamo Bay.

This leaves Renaissance: renaissance as conceived by Mahatma Gandhi (though I do not believe he used the term). People have to start doing their own thing. More and more (not least, via the internet) those foci of right-thinking, right-acting people might coordinate. Soon, the cadre of people worldwide doing sensible things would reach critical mass, and then we could start to create a world that is worth living in and has some chance of survival.

In *Feeding People is Easy*, I describe how this might be achieved in the context of food and agriculture – via what I call the Worldwide Food Club (WWFC), a cooperative of suppliers who give a damn, and seek only the opportunity to produce good food well; and of consumers willing to pay for what they produce. The WWFC would establish a trust, and that trust would acquire markets and farms of its own – owned by nobody except the collective trust.

Soon it could become a global player, able to rival the existing corporates and to out-flank their accessory governments, yet dedicated not to the mindless accumulation of wealth for ill-defined purposes, but to the well-being of humankind. In the short term, the WWFC could get away to a tremendous flying start just by bringing together all the many movements, great and small, that are moving in the right direction but not yet pulling together: the Slow Food movement, encouraging food culture; the organic movement, encouraging sound and humane husbandry; Compassion in World Farming; fair trade movements; various NGOs; farmers' markets; all the many farmers, butchers, brewers, cooks, bakers, and eaters who care about food; and indeed all those institutions and individuals who hold that justice and compassion are more important than short term power and cash.

I also envisage a 'College for Enlightened Agriculture' to provide the necessary intellectual base. Members of the college would constantly address the crucial issues that the present-day leaders of society have forgotten about – including Adam Smith's question: What proportion of people in any one society *should* be on the land? Or indeed: What are we trying to achieve, and why?

The general principle – people who know how things ought to be done and care about humanity and the world as a whole, just getting on and doing what needs doing despite the nonsense from above – could in principle spread beyond food and farming and into other fields: medicine, education, building. But food and farming seems to lend itself most readily to this kind of approach – and is also the thing we have to get right as a matter of urgency. The overall shape of governance in the end would not be the hierarchy, as at present, but a network – or rather a network of networks; a neural net. This, in a crowded world, seems the natural and the only plausible shape of democracy.

I think all this could be done. If it was, and it worked, it would at last put the world on a stable and agreeable footing. We could start with the Worldwide Food Club, backed up by the College for Enlightened Agriculture, and before long, good lives would not have to cost the Earth. Who would like to help that happen?

Rosie Boycott

All Life Depends on Plants

Sometime at the end of the 1990s I took my favourite aunt back to Jersey, in the Channel Islands, where she'd been born, my mother had been born and I'd been born. We went to visit the beach overlooked by the church in which we'd all been christened. It was also the beach where she had learnt to swim.

'We'd come down with a horse and a bathing wagon and then your mother and I would climb into the wagon which was towed out into the water by the horse. Then we'd climb down the little stairs at the back – instantly up to our necks in water. It was very modest and anyway, our bathing costumes reached our chins.'

When Giogia was a small child at the start of the twentieth century that was how life was. Now at the end of it, that world had become a distant place. We'd flown to the moon, invented the fax and the mobile phone, invented the internet and enabled people to fly all the way to Australia for as little as the price of a smart overcoat in a Bond Street store. Shops were full of produce from all over the world. Auntie Giogia just shook her head. Sometimes I find myself shaking mine: change is happening at an ever accelerating pace and we are now living through the most profound social and technological transformations history has ever seen.

We no longer seem to accept that anything can stay the same – indeed anything that does stay the same is viewed as a failure. In his brilliant book on the Shiants, the islands his father bought in the 1930s, Adam Nicolson recounts how for centuries the farmers were content to raise ten or so sheep on the poor rough grazing on the tiny islands. When the need for progress arrived on the Shiants, the then farmer decided to increase his herd to thirty. The result was predictable: there wasn't enough for the sheep to eat and within a few years the islands had been deserted, their age old tiny population relocated to the mainland where they could practise agriculture that grew. Sustainability – the buzz word of today – became a dirty word which marked the islands out as a failure.

Today we anticipate that things will change – almost constantly: that there will be a new cure for heart disease, there will be a faster car, a better sort of TV. Of course, so much of that change has been for the better: development and technology have provided comforts and benefits for everyone in the western world. Certainly the hazards of my aunt's young life – like crippling childhood diseases – are now, thankfully, things of the past. I have certainly grown up in a post-war era where I believed – completely automatically – that pretty much every change was a change for the good. Progress meant a step on the road to perfection and, like many of my generation, I think, I believed that science was essentially benign and that, in time, science would conquer all our problems.

But what I never questioned – and indeed didn't question until recently – was the basis for all this progress. At its most simple level, everything we have starts its life as part of the natural world. It is actually more simple even that that – everything really begins with a plant, or a root, or a leaf. Nothing in this world exists without the energy of the sun – that extraordinarily wonderful and complex process by which plants convert that energy into something that we can eat, or into something that we can use. So we take that energy either directly into ourselves by eating a carrot, or a little more indirectly by eating the cow which has eaten the grass which has converted the sun. Oil, laid down again, via plants, from the power of the sun, enables us to drive our cars, produce plastics, power our aeroplanes, live in a globalized world, go shopping down our local high street and buy a Barbie doll that has been made in China, use a computer whose many parts have been made from oil derivatives – the list is endless, and while the power of the sun may, indeed, be infinite, the earthly resources which it generates are anything but.

We have assumed that all this will be free and neverending. And this simple fact has been the driving force of our modern world and it is this fact that has brought us to the state we're in today. Because that rampant economic growth, built on high tech manufacturing, booming service sectors, fast food industries and the worldwide emergence of a consumer class are leading us – at a frightening speed – to ever growing demands for energy and natural resources – from oil and water to fish and timber.

Can we really carry on as we have been? My father was a Malthusian – and by that I mean that he firmly believed that the numbers of people on the planet, growing at such alarming rates, would spell the end of life as he knew it. When Christ was born there were just 200 million people on Earth. By 1500 there were 500 million. By 1825, there were a billion. By 1960, 3 billion, by 1975, 4 billion. By the time I saw in the new Millennium with my father, both of us leaning out of my window at Express Newspapers to watch the fireworks on the river Thames, there were 6 billion. Now, we're on the road to 9 billion.

He had some crazy ideas in his older years – shoot everyone over thirty-seven was one particularly draconian one that I recall – but think about it: can our planet support them all?

Because we have been lulled by the ever increasing brilliance of technology, most of us assume that we can. Because of our achievements, the popular assumption is that in order to feed everyone and make ourselves increasingly secure, we should – and can – just carry on. Taking everything out of the Earth that we can, hoping always to stay one step ahead of the moment of reckoning.

But the truth is, we can't. It's not just that the demands we are making on nature cannot be sustained, it's that in the process of all this progress we have created another, huge and overwhelming problem. Climate change.

Can anyone any more deny it? Just think of last spring. When we arrived to spend the Easter weekend in our cottage in Somerset, the countryside was still in the last grips of winter. The trees around our house – mostly oaks, field maples, some ash and some lovely old beeches were still – seemingly – lifeless, their branches still bare of leaf. On the ground, to be sure, spring was restlessly on the march: indeed the daffodils had flowered so early that many were now well past their peak and the prospect of dead-heading was what I thought awaited me in the garden over the week. As I drove down towards the west of England, through country which grows increasingly beautiful, spring was everywhere, in the primroses in the hedgerows, the white froth of blackwood blossom and the delicate green of the chestnut leaves as they unfurled themselves from their sticky buds.

By the time I tore myself away to come back to work and the city, just ten days later, I felt I'd lived through a speeded up transition, as though winter had given way not just to spring, but to early summer as well. I first noticed it in the trees: with three days of temperatures hovering in the late sixties, the first flush of leaf spread cautiously over the oaks. Then the field maple, which heralds the arrival of the new season by letting loose its miraculous electric green early leaves, burst into bloom. A week after Easter I went around the flower beds and wood, writing down the names of everything that was blooming, and it was astonishing.

The camellias were still showing their outer flowers, it is true, looking a bit worn after two months, but inside the thick bushes, I found flowers that seemed as fresh as the day they emerged. Near the wood was the yellow dog's-tooth violet, one of the world's most beautiful and delicate flowers, flowering at least four weeks ahead of time. There were tulips and daffodils, narcissi and magnolias, rhododendrons and tree peonies, flowering currants and bluebells. The list was endless. But strangest, possibly, of the lot was the sight of our wisteria, bursting into life on Easter Day, growing up the front wall of our house where it shares the space with three old rambling roses, two of which, a white and peach, had also come into flower. Beneath them, in the sheltered flowerbed, were tulips and hellebores (otherwise known as Christmas Roses because they do indeed flower after Christmas transforming a colourless January garden). If someone had painted a picture of all these flowers, blooming happily side by side, an astute and botanically-minded teacher would have been well within their right to chuck the drawing back as being 'quite impossible'.

It was a magical few days, as though we'd been transplanted into a speeded up world choreographed by David Attenborough to demonstrate how plants come to life. It was wonderful, but also very very worrying. The scientific evidence that has mounted up in recent years and the publication in 2006 of the Stern report, has left all but a few refuseniks convinced that global warming is happening. What we saw that week was a demonstration of how fast it may be happening. The effects that we will feel in this country will, in many respects, be ones we might welcome: shorter, warmer winters and longer summers which curtail our British spring. But for other countries the story will not be so pretty: droughts in Africa will means starvation for untold millions and sea level rises will drive millions more from their homes.

In 2007 the map of Greenland had to be redrawn. A new island has suddenly appeared off its coast, separated from the mainland by the melting of Greenland's enormous ice sheet. They've called it Warming Island.

From down here on the ground, the sky looks huge and neverending. How could humans – us tiny creatures buzzing around our daily business – actually affect something so big and fundamental as the weather? Yet, that sky is not as big as you might think. James Lovelock always says that, for him, the transformational moment came when he looked at the first pictures of our world, taken from space on those first *Apollo* missions. It looked beautiful and to him – a scientist with a keen mind and a great and compassionate heart – it also looked so fragile and vulnerable. Because in reality, the atmosphere which appears so limitless when we look upwards at the sky is actually no bigger than the equivalent of a coat of paint on a football. It's that small. It's that vulnerable. Most of the greenhouse gases that are causing our world to warm so dramatically are trapped in a layer of air about 6 miles thick. A distance even I could walk in a couple of hours.

And climate, as we are learning, is something that is finely poised and finely balanced. Lovelock called this space-around-the-world Gaia, something precious and extraordinary. It is self-contained and finely tuned: what happens in one place affects another.

Changes are undoubtedly happening. And the mechanism that causes them is called the enhanced greenhouse effect. Trap too many gases and the world warms and it is happening very very very fast . . . caused mainly by the large scale combustion of fossil fuels, which began in the Industrial Revolution with the burning of coal. It will – and is – causing large scale alterations to habitats, and already several species have been lost. According to the re-insurance giant, Munich Re, in 2005, climate change caused $200 billion of economic damage and about $75 billion of uninsured losses. People's welfare is also being undermined: billions of people now face water shortages, especially in countries like India where the rush to modernize means, for instance, the building of fast food chains across the country which use water by the bucket load. Water availability will hit food production. Diseases will spread. Last year, for the first time, the WHO revealed that more people had had to leave their homes because of climate change than political instability. In 2003 in Europe the unprecedented heat wave killed over 35,000 people. In Africa, 70 per cent of the population relies directly on rain-fed agriculture for their livelihoods. Now, season after season is rain free, crops are dying and people are being forced to leave their homes to try to survive. It is leading us, inexorably, towards what will be the greatest and most tragic flood of human movements, of refugees, that the world has ever known.

In his splendid book, *Six Degrees*, Mark Lynas charts what happens to the world with every degree Celsius of warming. Right now, we are .7 °C above pre-industrial averages and because of the damage already done, a further climb of .7 °C is now inevitable. If we pass the 2 °C point it is thought that irreversible feedback loops may kick in, making dramatically higher temperatures a certainty The discovery of Warming Island in 2005 is a signal of the increasing occurrence of positive feedbacks: melt some ice, there is less to reflect the heat, so the heat builds up and melts more ice. On and on. Unstoppable.

It is also, because this is the way of our world, horribly cruel. Because while we might like the warming weather, the people who will suffer most in a warming world are the poor of Third World countries, especially those in sub-Saharan Africa. In the 1990s, 600,000 people died in extreme weather events. It is making an unjust world much more unjust: after all, who burnt the fossil fuels in the first place?

If we are to do anything about all this we have to change. Not only do we have to treat the protection of the Earth as an issue of pressing urgency, but we must also take up the issue of environmental justice. Our relationship with the Earth is, I believe, a deeply moral matter: it has, in all its splendour, provided us with all the bounty that we have. It is very difficult too – we cannot say that developing countries must cease their development because the already-rich world has emptied the store cupboard.

We already have the technologies to start the transition out of the fossil fuel age. We know that politics and human will could bring about a huge transformation. Nearly two-thirds of the carbon dioxide in the atmosphere that is now causing climate change has been put there by the G8 countries, yet we have only 13 per cent of the world's population. It is therefore imperative the richest polluters must act first. It is no good us saying that as we, here in the UK, account for only 2 per cent of those emissions, that our efforts do not count. They do – for the simple reason that unless we act, there can be no leadership. The world needs an inspirational example to show that it is possible to reduce emissions while at the same time creating jobs and maintaining a sound economy and supporting a good quality of life.

Personally, I don't believe the politicians who say that we can do all this without changing our lifestyles. Yet, so far, there has been a lot of talk – with everyone agreeing – and precious little action. We're still shipping in blueberries from New Zealand, expanding airports like there's no tomorrow and Easyjet are planning on offering £7 flights to New York. Astonishingly, our airlines continue to pay no tax or VAT on fuel and – even more astonishingly – they are also exempt from the climate change levy, even though air travel is one of the most potent and fast growing sources of emissions.

I grew up in the 1960s and I became a feminist. We had a saying then and it was very important to us. It was that 'the personal is political'. How you live is just as important as what you say. We argued that by changing the way we lived, we would, in time, influence the larger world around us. Now, I think, that sentiment is back.

Since the war, we have demanded ever cheaper food, cheaper clothes, more holidays, more cars, more roads – a catalogue of mores and wants. It is this mind-set which has to change if we are truly going to shift the ethos and the politics and actually save what we have. Ultimately, it is the way we perceive the world and ourselves within it that determines how we behave. Change our perceptions and everything else will follow. But people ask 'what difference does it make if I bother to switch off that light, if I know that my neighbour is not bothering to switch off hers?' David Attenborough offered an answer when he came to make his first programmes about climate change:

> If you ask yourself what you might do in small ways, they may seem trivial. Turning off that light, not booking that aircraft seat when you could go by rail, even switching off the standby on your TV set. Trivial things, but what they add up to is a complete change of the way in which you view your life. It may seem odd at this particular moment for me to recall what it was like during the war, that you did not do things, not because you thought it was going to make a vast change, but because that was the way you looked at the world. It was a moral attitude: how we conduct our lives, how we look at energy and how we look at waste. I think it actually sinful to be wasteful.

Waste may seem an odd place for this argument to end up, but it actually says a great deal about how we are as a society. It is also an easy thing for us to change if we believe that our world's resources are limited. Nowadays we throw away almost one-third of the food we buy. For a typical family this means chucking out roughly £35 worth of food a week. 61 per cent of us regularly throw away lettuces, 60 per cent of us chuck out bread which is looking a bit hard, 57 per cent of us bin fruit, 45 per cent pour away milk and 43 per cent discard cooked meat. It is not just food that we throw away: our whole culture and our whole economic system is based on the notion of disposability and buying more.

Who needs just one packet of six hot-cross buns when you can have two for the price of one? Who needs just one bottle of sun-tan lotion, when you can get three for the price of two? Who on earth is going to bother to mend the iron when you can buy a new one for just £14.99? And where does my old iron go? Well, that's something that none of us really wants to know about. We produce 434 million tonnes of waste every year; that's a rate of generation that would fill the Albert Hall every two hours. On average each of us in the UK throws away seven times their body weight (about 500 kilogrammes) of rubbish every year. The nappies that are used by the average child in his or her lifetime weigh the same amount as the family car.

So why do we waste so much? Primarily because we are a rich society and if you're rich then you express your wealth through buying. We waste things precisely because we can. Advertising persuades us that we need new products that, by definition, displace the old ones. There is no cachet any longer in repairing things because nothing is designed with the future in mind. The lifespan of anything we buy is governed not by its usefulness, but by its fashion quotient. A workable mobile phone which doesn't take pictures is consigned to the bin so that we can have the latest model. The same is true of cars, clothes, kitchens, TVs, computers. While we believe that we must have the newest style available, we will continue to fill the landfill sites of Britain.

We believe, because we are told to, that possessions will make us happy, but this is only true up to a point. We are creatures of comparison and we only feel comfortable surrounded by people who have similar material possessions. When most people drove small cars, we could feel fine about ours. But when someone gets a BMW, the small car ceases to be something we like and becomes a symbol of the fact that we are not doing so well. The first person to have the BMW feels pretty good, but when everyone else has one too, then it begins to feel just like the small car. This mechanism, according to Nicholas Layard in his book *Happiness – Lessons from a New Science*, is what creates the paradox that, once basic needs are taken care of, rich societies are no happier than poor ones.

We need, he says, a psychological shift away from the mentality that assumes that everything we buy we will – sooner or later – throw away. One way, he suggests, is to encourage people to use their cash to buy services rather than products. The time-poor money-rich among us could think of sending their shirts away to be ironed, or we could join a car pool network rather than buying a second (or third) family car. Instead of being a society of instant gratification that needs new things to make us feel better right now, we need to find a way to shift our cultural outlook. Lord Haskins, Labour peer and former director of Northern Foods, says that the notion of buying something because you get an extra free, only to then put it in the bin, is a cultural thing, a sort of greed. Stuff – in all its forms – fills the empty spaces inside which materialism creates.

I know, intellectually, that stuff doesn't buy me happiness, yet throughout my adult life, I've bought things as much for the momentary buzz of acquisition as from any real need. Much of it, in time, will be thrown away. If everyone in the world consumed as much and created as much waste as the average person in the UK we would need the resources of eight new worlds to support us.

It is unrealistic to imagine that we could ever live in a world where there was zero waste, but in September 2001, the Bath and North East Somerset council became the first British local authority to adopt such a policy. On their website they said:

> Zero waste is a concept that is spreading throughout the globe. Our vision is to reduce consumption of goods by ensuring that products are made to be reused, repaired or recycled. What we now call waste should be regarded as a mixture of resources to be used again to their full potential, not as something to be thrown away.

As Al Gore says in his brilliant film, *An Inconvenient Truth*, climate change does not have to be the end of everything we know, rather it could be the making of us all.

5

Good Designs

Through his television programme *Grand Designs* and associated publications **Kevin McCloud** has become a figurehead in the movement for a better and more sustainable built environment. But his interests are much broader than that. 'I'm intrigued by the idea of readopting principles such as thrift, and by leading slower lives, such as with the Italian slow food movement, and walking just a little bit more and playing more,' he says. Many in the green movement, he argues, could do themselves a favour by 'Celebrating good times and drinking good organic local beer', and, ultimately, we need to rediscover the art of delight: 'I think there's a lot to be said for what's laughably called the simple pleasures, as they are actually quite sophisticated pleasures.' McCloud says we must beware 'greenwash' and is appalled at the lack of progress in the building industry and planning system. If design and architecture is to help us create places in which good lives are more possible, we must stop talking about building homes that are more environmentally friendly. We have known how to do that for decades. Instead we need to start thinking about how to build real communities.

Red or Dead, the famous fashion label, was founded by **Wayne Hemingway**. He is now renowned for redesigning more than just clothes. Now the challenge of mass housing projects is his main line of work. It's a long way from selling summer dresses on Camden Market in London in 1981. Wayne argues that we need to rediscover the value of durability, 'one of the highest qualities which traditional manufacturing used to pride itself in', in all the goods that we make. Shocked by what he saw while working in Dubai where 'the average building is designed to last approximately eighteen years at most', he concludes that we must promote the 'best of the old-fashioned principles of thrift and durability but without taking the fun out of people's lives'.

Outspoken design guru **Stephen Bayley** is passionate about beautiful things. But he is equally passionate in his dislike for windmills. In this essay he strikes a very different tone to other contributors and tilts at this manifestation of renewable energy with the eagerness of a latter day Don Quixote. He finds all that is wrong with our response to environmental concerns engrained in the quietly turning blades of the modern day wind turbine. 'Everywhere we go there are signs and portents of the impending eco catastrophe,' writes Bayley, 'and our, occasionally desperate, attempts to fend it off.' On a more upbeat note, he believes that, 'We are slowly emerging from a culture of waste.' Good design can make a huge contribution to turning around a society hooked into wasteful disposability. He asks, 'If something is well designed, if something is beautiful, why would you ever want to throw it away?'

Nic Marks, founder of the *Centre for Well-Being* at nef, has been playing with numbers for as long as he can remember. Maths was his refuge at school. He could always see better through a numeric lens than one made of historical fact or literary flight. Here, Nic shows how at the end of a circuitous journey, his love of numbers resulted in a new way of seeing the economy. Instead of relying on abstract financial and economic data, with some help from his friends and colleagues he came up with something far more telling – a measure of the efficiency with which natural resources are turned into long and happy lives.

Kevin McCloud

(in conversation with Andrew Simms)

The Re-attraction of Delight

Q: The very words design and designer have been co-opted and associated with expense and high cost. Can notions of good design and thrift ever go together?

You've touched on a very, very interesting nerve. It is the nub of what I want to explore in the relationships between design and the made world, and between value and materialism. There are real distinctions to be made. The word design has become synonymous with the words *fashion, trend* and *styling,* all of which have insinuations of temporality, i.e., 'it's gone tomorrow'. These are all very fleeting. I come at the issue as a designer and as someone who works with architects and the design process.

To me design is a process. It's something we all do every day without thinking. 'Trend' architects use that particular process and are used to quick collaboration. Design is about collecting and researching, going out and looking for things. Then bringing them back, honing and sorting through, and applying all that information to a context, a brief, and trying to satisfy the demands of that brief in as elegant a way as possible. It's fair to say that most designers and architects get up in the morning with the desire to make the world a better place.

What I see is a predominately man-made world; I see fields and trees, but many hundreds of years ago they were fenced, and planted and channelled and dug. I champion the design process as a process that makes us want to get out there and improve the world and the environment and make it more satisfying. It's misleading to think of the future of the world or the environment or sustainability or the future of the planet, or rather the natural world, as something regressing to a point pre-15,000 years ago. We have to find ways of making arcs so that we can satisfy human desires for improvement and enjoy our human passion for making things, and we have to do that at the same time as having regard to resources and how we damage the place we inhabit, a place that has just a thin veil of atmosphere and finite resources.

Design is about whether we're going to put this tie with this shirt, or whether we're going to drive this way to work or take a train. And these are decisions about suitability, about appropriateness, about your lifestyle, your taste and aesthetics. The difference between us and a trained architect is that an architect has lots and lots of skills whereby he can prod and weed and poke and extract different bits of information from a bag full of detail and come up with a view of the world that's much more fully formed than it was before.

What is interesting is the way in which the implications of the word design are tarted up. If you look at car manufacture, for instance, a big part of car design is actually styling. It is of its time and period and this has a value. These are often objects of great beauty and great craftsmanship. And, when you talk to an engineering designer about the engine that goes into that car, into the braking system, they are fascinated by this idea of efficiency and elegant solutions, and creating something that has minimal workings, minimal embodied energy, which is a simple device that does a clever thing.

So, it's important when you're talking about being environmental and the sustainable impact of design, to disassociate that which is very temporary and transient from that which has some kind of lasting value. And to have lasting value it doesn't need to last for ever; it can have a lasting cultural value, like a 1937 Alfa Romeo has a lasting cultural value in terms of the design and body style. You could argue that style is superficial. But there is permanent tension between style and design. You have to evaluate the contributions of these disciplines separately, I think – in terms of their overall cultural contributions, and in terms of their lasting effect, and in terms of their efficiency and their elegance as well.

Q: You said that the future will not be built on the foundations of nostalgia for a golden age which, in any case, probably never existed. But can you think of any examples of a particular time or age when people made successful choices to pare things down to their elegant essentials?

I think you can look at the history of design and architecture as a series of attempts for each generation to rewrite the language of design and to develop that language. And sometimes in a particular generation you find an evolutionary approach which is very eclectic and which becomes very wide-ranging and develops, for example, into a style like Georgian architecture and decoration and can be very satisfying as a result.

And there are other times where you find that social upheaval and even revolution causes a great change, and with that often comes a reappraisal. But sometimes with that comes a great repression too. And for every period of repression, there is often a period of immense excitement and liberation that follows. For example, in the twentieth century you can equate modernism within Europe, France and Germany with Bauhaus, and an approach to design that was very, very pared back. It was about stripping away decoration, and finding the functionality in buildings and in objects, and pure ergonomics as a satisfying experience. And that was in reaction to the gross exuberance of early twentieth-century decoration and design, which became exuberant to the point of being clumsy and uncomfortable. But the Arts and Crafts movement in the mid-nineteenth century did have a fair stab at working with 'elegant essentials'. In the 1950s, after the Second World War, in the UK and in Europe, and America in the sixties, you find not exactly a reaction to modernism, but a very fast evolution of design that was quite celebratory.

I have a particular favourite period, which is the British Commonwealth. It was a time of great religious and social austerity and led to the creation of a decorative and architectural style, which was in itself quite pared back. For example the silver of the period is remarkably simple and looks almost 1950s. It has a great, almost modernist minimalism to it. It's interesting to see how that compares to Queen Anne or Jacobean silver. It's very austere and rather beautiful and very much to contemporary taste.

Today, there is a slightly unpalatable movement to try and reintroduce principles of forced austerity and simplicity among people who are opting out and choosing the simple life. It's one thing to start to grow your own vegetables, travel less, not go to the West Indies, not fly, work at home, and consume less. But that's very different to deciding that you're going to adopt some kind of austere and terrifyingly humble approach to life. If we're not careful we're going to end up with another reformation. It's important to realize that what humans actually need, and architecture is only just getting to grips with, is the idea of delight.

Joy and delight are two very under-used words, as indeed is beauty, except of course in certain magazines. In terms of our physical environment, I think that they have been missing for a very long time, apart from in a brief phase in the 1950s. I'm not sure that I see puritanism as a kind of constant evolution but I do see that in a poly-cultural society, it's always there, trying to make its mark all the time. All the great religious movements and philosophies of the world have never, ever, been as successful as materialism. Materialism is the one great cultural ethos that everybody has latched on to and enjoys.

But, although we all enjoy material pursuits, many of them are deeply unsatisfying, and all the great satisfying experiences of life are free. The great danger is that puritans latch into this and promote the idea that we can live in a non-consumer society. I can't quite see that. Human beings consume, human beings breathe air, we produce tens of thousands of litres of CO_2 every year and just by being here we damage the planet, regardless of whether we go shopping on Oxford Street. Sustainability is about refocusing.

I'm intrigued by the idea of readopting principles such as thrift, and by leading slower lives, such as with the Italian slow food movement, and walking just a little bit more and playing more. Celebrating good times and drinking good organic local beer – I think there's a lot to be said for what's laughably called the simple pleasures, as they are actually quite sophisticated pleasures.

I have a thing about beer. I don't go to pubs much, but I do like a drink of beer. I went to a pub in the next village and they had ten different types of cider. I live in Somerset and most of the beer on offer came from Hereford and Ireland. They had fifteen lagers from all over Europe and one beer from Yorkshire, John Smith's. We have ten breweries within 20 miles and I thought, where are their bottles? So why is it that people are not interested, why do they not want that connection with place? Is it that we feel more glamorous drinking a German beer brewed in a giant chemical works in Aachen than we do drinking something local from the place where we grew up? What happened to our pride of place, what happened to our sense of connection to place?

Q: Britain has a major new building programme with 3 million new houses planned. What advice would you give to the

*Government and developers so that we end up with environ-
mentally-friendly homes and convivial communities?*

I'm working in Swindon on a development building 400 homes
on two different sites. One of the issues people raise is how you
make homes both green and affordable. I was asked to go to a
conference recently, the title of which was, 'How do we build
sustainably?'; and I didn't go because I thought it was a complete
waste of my time. Just stop asking that question, we know how
to do it – all over Europe people have been doing it for thirty or
forty years. We know how to build relatively affordably and
sustainably, that's not the issue, we know how to do it. The issue
is how do we make places, how do we make communities, out of
new houses, on greenfield sites, that don't harm the biodiversity
of that place, and that create a sense of local identity and
uniqueness. It's a hard question, but the key to the answer is very
simple, and that is, you employ good architects, you employ
good designers, you use the design process which responds to
place and context just as much as it responds to people.

Norman Foster said that it takes 200 years to make a place,
and in a sense it does. Because the resonance of place comes
from the over-layering of culture, of human occupation,
enmarkment and the landscape. It's very satisfying, for
instance, to go to a place like Bath, or Edinburgh or Bury St
Edmunds and see the building languages of those places, or
somewhere like Paris, where the building languages are
unique to the place, in terms of materials, and all the other
cultural, environmental and historical influences. It's very
satisfying to find a 'history of use' for the place.

So my advice to the Government would be first to have the
right building regulations and make buildings truly sustainable. It's a much bigger issue than just using green materials,
it's about how that community functions, and how it uses its
resources in the long term. That's what the major difference
would be, not whether you use an environmental concrete

block, or a straw bale to build your house with. In a way those issues are far less relevant because the resources that go into the place are far outnumbered by the impact of the resources the community uses over the longer term. Consequently, it's important to make places that are unique and strong so that people want to stay there, so that it doesn't degenerate, and people take pride in their surroundings, they connect. So I think that making places that are rich, are powerful, are truly sustainable, is the first thing.

The second point is that you've got to use architects. The design cost of the average new-build house is about £200. When you think how much it costs to buy it, and that's how much goes towards design, it's ludicrous. We should be using fine architects, we should be building 'in time of mind' to quote John Lennon, we should be constructing architecture which has a powerful contemporary resonance, and responds to people as they live now and as we think they will live in the future. That's important.

The third thing is highlighted by what we face at our development in Swindon. We've got 500 acres, and the town has a masterplan which often means, in effect, chopping down every tree and removing every hedge so as to start with a blank sheet of paper and create a new community. My argument is, no, historically agriculture has just as important a role in shaping landscape as housing does. Let's start with our field boundaries and our landscapes and hedges and streams and let's work with that, and let's actually create housing that responds to that and which somehow fits. I'm not saying they are going to be hobbit homes, they will be contemporary buildings, but which respect the history of the place and the history of the use of the place as well. They will add another layer, and, importantly, with every layer that we add we should allow the previous layer to read though it. That's what I mean when I talk about resonance.

My other point to the Prime Minister, Gordon Brown, is that we are in the midst of this extraordinary phase of construction at the moment that involves the most terrible demolition. On my desk, I have just received six letters that ask me to help support them against planning schemes in town centres. One of them, for instance, is against two town centre schemes that are going to demolish two Art Deco cinemas in Aldershot. They are probably the only two Art Deco buildings in Aldershot. If you remove those, what are you left with? – a town that's minus a stripe of its own history. You're turning it into anywhereville and it becomes another anonymous clone town.

People just don't get it. I've been part of a campaign to retain a beautiful 1930s Bath Stone façade and Bath Stone building, and they were turned into something else and it's all gone half-cocked. It's another beautifully made 1920s building which represented a period that was really under-represented in Bath and you felt that it was an important contribution to the history of the place. Lose it, and you've lost it, you've lost it completely, and you're left with something that will be pulled down in twenty years' time. That's how we're building at the moment, and I think we're in great danger of damaging irrevocably our existing towns and cities, and we're in great danger of building new ones which show a scant regard for history and for sense of place and for resonance. That would be my third point.

Q: Do you see any significant, positive changes happening in the building industry, is there ground for hope?

No, what I see is increasingly industrialized construction methods that build everything faster, a planning system that is now veering in favour of the large-scale developer, large-scale infrastructure and housing projects and power stations, and slight backtracking on important out-of-town zoning.

Five years ago we were in a stronger position in terms of the planning of our towns and cities than we are now, at least in terms of policy. I think that we've done better on housing, but I think that the wider planning issues are still not resolved. There are lots of guidelines and voluntary codes, and lots of good things coming from groups like English Partnerships and CABE (the Commission for Architecture and the Built Environment). But, in terms of creating new towns, I don't think anyone has really grasped the nettle and embraced fine architecture, sustainability and the importance or sensitivities of the historical place. You've got to be able to take all of those ideas and bag them to start making an interesting new town.

Q: What are the obstructions to progress?

We have a suspicion of design, a suspicion of architects, of architecture – and architects have been partly to blame for that – but I think that architecture now is a completely different discipline, a different kind of mould. Many architects now are highly urbane and really do care about the decisions they make, and about the environment in a wider way. I detect much less arrogance and much more willingness to investigate, to have fun and deliver. I think we're beginning to deliver some really fine architecture.

And there is *some* good central Government policy. But the trouble is there is just so much policy, and it changes so often, that local authorities cannot move fast enough to implement it or even understand it. The planning system has a way to go, its structure needs to be beefed up and changed. What we're lacking is not guidelines but the right culture. One of the most damaging things to happen in the last ten years has been the creation of the Department for Culture, Media and Sport (DCMS) and the integration of heritage into the DCMS as basically an adjunct along with museums. Every village, every community, every place in Britain has its heritage, and that's what makes these places exciting to be and live in.

You can't legislate for that, you need to value it, in the way that the Italians value their public sphere. The French are better also, but the British, we just haven't got it, we just haven't got or understood that relationship between history and between sustainability and architectural design. We pursue one at the expense of the others, when you've got to integrate them all to make sense. I keep coming back to this great magic, this great triangle of these three things, and they indeed are the three things that I want to talk to Gordon Brown, the Prime Minister, about.

Q: The only open space in my town centre is a supermarket car-park, but in Italy or France the same ground would probably be an attractive town square. Do we no longer understand the value of public space?

First of all what we're losing is the small trader, and it's why I'm very keen on the local, because it encourages small local retailers to populate towns and communities and cities. When you turn a corner and find a street of local shops, it's a delight.

You find it still, in towns and cities. It's not that the Italians have it and we haven't. It's just a question of how we create the fertile environment for it to happen, and we have a fairly crude retail policy. You'll get a planning application to do a mixed scheme, with offices over the top of shops, and what that has meant is shopping arcades which at night are no-go areas. At the Bullring in Birmingham, which has a very big shopping centre, they have now put in flats. I'm not saying it's a perfect solution, but it's better than not having urban centres lived in.

Good architecture and design is about the space between the buildings, as much as it is about the buildings themselves. Good contextual response architecture incorporates that. I'm not a fan of 'look at me' architecture, but I think Norman Foster's very good at that. If you take the example of the Gherkin, this actually responds rather brilliantly to where it is, and that's a great art.

Q: I want to ask how bold you think are the claims that can be made for architecture, can good buildings help give people good lives?

The easiest way to answer the question, does good architecture improve people's lives, is to reverse the question and ask, does bad architecture damage people's lives? And I think that's so self-evident as to make the answer to the first question obvious.

Of course, if you walk into a building with low ceilings, dark and cramped, it's not going to make you feel good. Generally, human beings are taller than they are wide, we're very tactile creatures, we like to touch things and hold things and we respond to comfort and we respond to subtle changes in temperature. We enjoy a breeze on a summer's evening. We find these things pleasurable experiences. And if you can bring these ideas into a building, it's generally going to make you feel good.

Whereas if you work in a building that has few changes of air per hour, that has closed air-conditioning and where you can't hear the birds sing, you're going to feel worse than being in a building where you can hear the birds sing, or even hear the traffic. There are plenty of examples where workers have been moved to new buildings where the windows opened, and people turned up for work more, and they didn't get so poorly.

It's also the small details that matter: generous, gratuitous door handles that people want to touch, a view of the sky through to infinity, and what an architect friend of mine calls the 'naked view' – a window at home in front of which she slept naked all day. Funnily enough, these are simple pleasures again, the feeling of a breeze on your skin and touching something that's pleasurable, and looking at something that's satisfying and a feeling of being slightly taller, slightly better, slightly happier, because the building respects you.

The same is true if you go to a public building and find that the front door is obvious and welcoming, and when you walk in, the building smiles at you and isn't too forbidding. Then there are the buildings which are easy to navigate and which play little theatrical tricks on you, taking you into a confined area and then releasing you into a big open space, the ones that appear to float perhaps, defy gravity, suggest something rather magical.

Notably, if you live or work in a building that does these things, you feel proud that someone designed and built it for you. You feel lucky. Architecture can have all kinds of positive effects.

A great building is a building that makes you feel like a better human being. You walk in and think, yeah, wow. You leave your cares outside. The building enwraps you and protects you and enhances you.

Q: In an age of climate change, it's typically much more carbon-efficient to renovate existing buildings than to build new ones from scratch. Should we be putting more effort into rehabilitating the houses we already have and bringing empty properties back into use, before we carpet-bomb the landscape with new buildings?

The issue of maintenance is very interesting. The other day I saw a very beautiful Austin Montego and it was pristine, they obviously polished it every day and kept it in the garage. And I thought, I really admire that car, and I don't know why as I laugh at every other Montego. It was because it was so beautiful, it was cherished and polished and pristine. And it's the same with buildings, we leave them for thirty, forty years, they get a bit of rust in the framework, the paint peels and the windows go rotten, and what do people want to do, they want to tear them down.

I work with the World Wide Fund for Nature, whose next big campaign is the retro-fit of existing homes and empty dwellings for greater energy efficiency. Shelter, the charity for the homeless, identified this huge number of empty dwellings and the building research establishment, having figured out the kind of technologies we should use for new-build, are now addressing how we retro-fit existing buildings. But of course, as ever, the Germans have beaten us to it. Angela Merkal has committed billions to bring every home in Germany up to high energy efficiency standards. It isn't just low carbon, its zero carbon, without using any form of heating. As usual, we'll faff around for five or ten years trying to get it right, only to find the answer lay across the Channel all the time. Do you want to know the answer of how to build sustainably? Go to Germany. Look around. There are four housing estates I can send you to in Germany that are ultra-low carbon if not zero or positive carbon, and take into account all other issues of sustainability and resource management. It's all happening over there while we pootle on in our insular little way.

Q: Personally, what gives you your greatest sense of well-being?

Planting trees, which I do a great deal of and which I didn't start doing for any ecological reason. I started planting trees because I love gardening and because I discovered that with a small farm I could find a greater contact with the earth, with the place where I am, by just standing in the middle of a field.

My favourite trees are deciduous – oak, ash, anything that doesn't die on me. I'm very fond of alder, it's beautiful, and it grows very well here in Somerset. I still walk and climb.

Spending a day planting trees in a field is a similar kind of physical pleasure to walking or climbing a mountain. I've been at home on the farm and I've looked up and seen five deer or a stag run across the field in front of me in the mist, in the dew, in the early morning, and things like that are an extraordinary fortune. What more do you want? Well, there's playing with my children obviously. I spend my life travelling, so when I come home I really like to nestle in and hunker down and put a flat cap on and go out and be a farmer and break the ground.

Q: Do good lives have to cost the Earth?

Inside the tube of an eco-light bulb is a host of electronics and mercury, and phosphors from heavy metals and electronics containing stuff like iridium, a metal which is going to run out in fifteen years, and we have to find a replacement or we'll have no electronics. So where does that leave us? Is this an eco-bulb? If not, do I have to have paraffin lamps, how far does it have to go, do I have to grow my own rape seed for fuel oil?

For me, the great dilemma, the great danger, is that we pursue the quick fix. If we're not careful we'll go down this terrible, utilitarian, shaker route, where we'll all end up being dour, ethically-shrunken miserabilists. And I dread that. And on the other hand, we may find ourselves very sanctimoniously declaring in ten years' time that we all use eco-bulbs and we're all driving around on bio-fuels, and our carbon impacts may be reduced but it'll be at the expense of other resources and other impacts on the planet.

I think that what's required is an enormous amount of intellectual application and an enormous amount of creativity. And I believe that human beings are capable of this. But we are nowhere near that level of input from our great minds to this problem, to solving the great mysteries of how we

sustain our existence happily, and how we develop a sym-
biotic relationship with the planet. We are not going to do it
by becoming happy-clappy, hair-shirt wearing miserabilists.
We are not going to do it by succumbing to greenwash – and
greenwash can be extremely sophisticated.

I think that human beings are of our own environment, we
are the problem but we are also the solution: the cause and
the cure and also the patient. If our environment is damaged
to the extent that we cannot survive in it, we will die, we'll be
wiped out. And in 200 years the planet will regenerate as a
perfect Eden. So the planet won't suffer, the planet is not
doomed. If it all goes badly wrong, mankind is doomed – and
maybe polar bears. But the planet will develop a new ecosystem after it. So we are the problem, we are the patient and the
victim, we are the potential solution. And the solutions, I
think, as they come, when they come, will be creative and
breathtaking, and not all to do with technology. Some of
them will be cultural change and the pursuit of different
happinesses and joys. I look for that kind of re-attraction of
delight. If people are happier, they want less.

I'm writing about a series of personal journeys. Not just
physical journeys, but physical, emotional and intellectual,
about design. It's about trying to find this path that we collectively have to tread, and it's an appeal for intellectuality, an
appeal for creativity and an appeal to bring the power of great
minds to bear on the issue.

A lot of what I'm trying to do is to take the idea of one-
planet living and evolve it. For me, it's about trying to bring
together these ideas of sustainability and community and
trying to join them to find a rounded approach to how we
treat our environment.

Wayne Hemingway

Designed to Last

I was born in the seaside town of Morecambe, Lancashire and until my Mum met my step-Dad and we moved inland to Blackburn, we lived with my Nan and Pop – Ida and Colin.

The Hemingways were a working class, Yorkshire family – Nan had moved to Morecambe for health reasons – thrifty and careful. Nan and Pop died a decade ago and I miss them dearly, but I can still taste the veg that Pop grew in their tiny back garden, the fruit he grew in his home-made greenhouse, the stews that Nan made in Pyrex casserole dishes that were clean but ingrained from thirty years of cooking the same stewing steak and onions. I can smell the homely smell of sofas, cushions and rugs that had served them well since the fifties, and my school butties wrapped in old Co-op bags and sealed in Tupperware.

Money was short, but you wouldn't have thought so from the way we all looked. My Mum and Nan always looked wonderfully cool in their printed summer dresses, all made on the sewing-machine in the back room that seemed to whirr away non-stop. They were the same summer dresses that Geraldine and I sold on Camden Market back in 1981, and that got our business going. Nan would sit knitting jumpers and mitts for me from patterns passed down from her Mum.

I continued this thrifty upbringing into adulthood. There is always a use for old plastic bags (what's the point of bin liners?). Bags of compost may be cheap but home-made compost saves the odd fiver and, as my Mum always says, 'If you watch the pennies the pounds will always look after themselves.' The old sit-up-and-beg fifties rust-bucket of a bike that I first bought when I moved to London in 1979 is still my preferred mode of city transport (who needs gears in a flat-ish city, and who's going to nick a bike that chavs laugh at?).

Has there been a better men's shirt produced than those three-pocket, open-neck sports shirts sold by M&S, C&A, BHS and the like? I clearly don't think so: I've collected more than fifty over the years in various shades. And how can you walk out of a room and leave the light on? My kids know that you can but it costs them a 50 pence fine every time they do.

I didn't buy my Toyota Prius three years ago because some Californian celebs had one; it was because of the emissions issue, but also because I can get over 70 miles to the gallon. My early introduction to thrift and my lifelong adherence to thrifty principles happily make me sustainable. Once I was considered 'tight-arsed': now the media come to me to discuss environmental issues.

I often get asked by the media for my favourite design classics, and my answers are often taken as ironic, but they are far from it. With my background, is it likely that I would put a £1,000 chair or a daft sputnik-like lemon squeezer at the top of my list?

What I do appreciate are durable designs that do a job and save money. My favourite household object must be the rotary-airer. No matter how small the space outside your home, there is room for this fold-up baby. The four-arm version gives you enough feet of line to let the breeze go to work on four large bath towels, two face cloths, a headscarf, two knitted jerkins, a twin-set, three pairs of slacks, a dozen pairs of underpants or knickers (or combination of the two), ten pairs of socks, six brassieres, a pair of long johns, various tea towels depicting holiday destinations or the British royal family, a set of king size bedsheets and a selection of babygrows.

Looking around my house, it is full of products that have stood the test of time, yet are unheralded. Simple tin-openers, folding deckchairs, garden tools passed down from Pop, spanner sets bought at car boot sales . . . the list goes on. Durability was one of the highest qualities which traditional manufacturing used to pride itself in, but it has been forsaken in favour of fashionable gimmicks and fast turnaround. We are entering an exciting new era, I hope, where we are prepared to demand that durability be put back on the agenda as an essential ingredient for sustainability.

I've just spent some time working in the United Arab Emirates and was shocked to find that Dubai has absolutely no concept of recycling or, for that matter, durability. It's normal there to change your car every year, and the average building is designed to last approximately eighteen years at most. When I was there, I gave a talk at a design conference. I think they were expecting me to talk about flashy design and praise the shiny new buildings, but I just said how much I hated it. The whole ostentatiousness of it is a bit frightening.

Part of the problem with Government trying to communicate about sustainability and environmental issues generally is that it's all just a bit too politically correct. It's important to get the message across without preaching – and especially not just preaching to the converted, as so many of these Government initiatives do. In a way, I'm all for making an example of people who refuse to recycle, and we need to confront the situation head-on a bit more. But we also need to be more creative about it and work out what, and who, pushes people's buttons.

We can't change the fact that new things stimulate us. But if we really are to achieve sustainability, then durability is incredibly important. The second-hand culture isn't nearly as strong here as it is, for instance, in western Australia and other parts of the world.

In my main line of work, looking at mass housing projects, the industry is under pressure and desperately trying to be more sustainable in terms of energy use and emissions. But what could be more sustainable than building houses like the Victorians, Georgians and Edwardians did, who have all bequeathed us homes that the public cherish, are highly adaptable and are still more popular than most new housing. Surely the most sustainable thing that society can do is produce goods like Victorian housing that go on and on and on and on and ...

In terms of what makes a good life, it's essentially about being with the people you love to have around. I've never been a loner and the biggest wrench I could possibly imagine would be not to have the people I am close to around me.

I'd be lying if I said it was only about that – one of the best things that ever happened to me when the business took off was being free from money worries, being able to take the kids out of school and having the time and the freedom to be more creative, which was much harder when we were struggling financially. At the same time, we didn't just instantly change the way we lived and run around spending loads of money – we stayed true to our thrifty principles. Being successful was never about the money as such, but more about quality of life and being in a position where we were free to do what we wanted.

Basically, it's about pushing forward the best of the old-fashioned principles of thrift and durability but without taking the fun out of people's lives.

Stephen Bayley

Tilting at Windmills

Fairtrade coffee. Israeli strawberries in December. A fug of superheated steam from the condensers of the Mitsubishi aircon in the building opposite. A howling jet on final approach bashing and chewing molecules of God's good air. Strange, silent, plastic cars. Strange, noisy, wind farms. The standby tell-tale on the HDTV anathematized. Blue plastic bags. Orange plastic bags. Green plastic bags. Black plastic bags. No plastic bags. Everywhere we go there are signs and portents of the impending eco catastrophe and our, occasionally desperate, attempts to fend it off.

We are slowly emerging from a culture of waste. On my very first visit to Dallas-Fort Worth airport nearly thirty years ago, I stepped blinking out of the aeroplane and looked at the sun-baked car-park. It was full of Cadillacs, many of them pink, many of them enhanced in their congenital kitsch by the addition of steer's horns on the front of the bonnet. All of them were empty and all of them had been left with their big lazy old technology V8s rumbling at tick-over. I asked my host what was going on. He explained that Texans like to leave their engines running so the air-conditioning stays working so that, after a meal of Coors and transfats, they can step straight into a behemoth car as cold as a chest freezer and do some drunk-driving.

But now even the grossest Texans are having a fit of revisionism. The reluctance of American consumers to buy heavy, inefficient American vehicles has driven General Motors and Ford to the rim of the abyss.

Only a fool would be complacent: there is still a lot of tidying-up to do, still a lot of greedy habits that need to be tamed, yet more economies to be made, new disciplines to be established, but it is important not to become hysterical about environmental doom. The answer to the world's problems is not less technology, but cleaner, better, more intelligent technology. Take Formula One. Those antic polychrome cars we see every other weekend during the season may seem an affront to sanity, but they in fact present exemplary models of efficiency to inspire all manufacturers. There are plans that the rules governing Formula One should be changed so that each team starts the season with a certain amount of green credit and that, as fuel is burnt and rubber is worn, that credit is consumed. So there will be a huge competitive incentive to become yet more efficient. Rules, as Sir Joshua Reynolds knew, stimulate genius.

Or take architecture. Already sensible architects are designing houses with recycled materials and a view to sustainability. But this does not mean we are all going to have to live in rude structures made of compounded hemp, lit by tallow and irrigated by insanitary grey water. On the contrary, the most interesting new building material is a timber product called Eurban. This ingeniously uses the residue from the conventional operation of turning tree trunks into planks. But the great thing is Eurban is not a product that diminishes the prospects for interesting architecture: on the contrary, it enhances them. Eurban is thermally efficient, environmentally responsible, pleasing to the eye and, best of all, has structural properties that allow architects to design adventurous and imaginative spaces that would be unfeasibly expensive in steel. Similarly, there is a big future for plant-based plastics.

Man is *homo faber*, a divine monkey who makes tools. While saving the planet is a priority no one should ignore, it's important to remember that since we stepped out of the primeval glop on to the dry shore and started the journey that ended with reality TV, the world has been constructed by us. What we call the countryside is, in fact, an industry. Field patterns, enclosures, hedgerows, irrigation systems are all evidence of the systematic and pitiless subjugation of nature to anthropoid needs. There was no agriculture in Eden. What's now needed for survival is ingenuity . . . and a refusal to make lazy, defeatist, anti-technological solutions in pursuit of an Elysium that never was.

Now, take windmills: primary evidence of this industrialization of nature. Readers of Carlo Ginzburg's *Il formaggio e i vermi* (*The Cheese and the Worms*, 1976), an astonishing account of a mad miller from Friuli who reckoned the cosmos had its origin in putrefaction, will find it difficult to maintain a sentimental attitude to the culture of mills of any sort, but not so the rest of us. These mighty engines designed to exploit zephyrs, to grind and to pump for profit, retain a theoretical, magical charm. Daudet's *Lettres de Mon Moulin* (*Letters from my Windmill*,1869) is a rural masterpiece. Windmills seem innocent, offering vistas of escape.

And there is a new generation of windmills, no longer grinding and pumping, but saving the planet with energy that's not just cheap . . . but free. Or so they say. So with a pleasant culture of associations behind them and the prospect of clean energy in front of them, why do the new WTGs (Wind Turbine Generators) cause so much controversy and unease? Well, for a start, Cervantes sensed the unnatural menace of all windmills. The world's favourite delusional *caballero de la triste figura* says to Sancho Panza:

Look there where thirty or more monstrous giants rise up, all of whom I mean to engage in battle and slay, and with whose spoils we shall begin to make our futures. For this is righteous warfare and it's God's good service to sweep so evil a breed from the face of the earth.

This is exactly the response in Europe and America – from the Scottish Highlands and Islands to Nantucket – when an authority (it is always an authority) proposes a wind farm. Instead of exciting enthusiasm, everybody wants, like Don Quixote, to tilt at Wind Turbine Generators. Even technophiles find wind farms disturbing. One of Europe's biggest is built on the high ground of the Cortijo de la Joya above Tarifa in southern Spain. This magical part of Andalucia is swept by the levante and the tramontana, winds Odysseus knew. And the spectral sight of the Danish contractor's WTGs spooling away like the Don's monstrous giants is appalling. They seem remote and threatening, disturbingly proportioned, inhumane and a source of sinister noise. Sometimes a whistle, more often a thwuck-thwuck-thwuck like a CH-47 Chinook heavy-lift helicopter coming in to land on your patio.

And there are environmental as well as aesthetic reasons for objecting too. Unscrupulous operators in the United States are planting wind farms in exactly the same rapacious land-grab style of ranchers and oilmen. In 2003 2,000 bats were killed by the forty-four WTGs at Thomas, West Virginia. Conservationists were horrified when an early wind farm on the Altamont Pass in California turned rare raptors and owls into terrine. The awkward fact is that the windy parts of the world are often the most beautiful and most sensitive to desecration. The 24 square mile wind farm planned for Nantucket Sound will have 134 100-foot high WTGs.

Part of the problem with wind farms is that whenever the environment is discussed, people leave their brains behind. In his marvellously contrarian book *Why Things Bite Back* (1996), Edward Tenner described a concept known as the Revenge Effect (a version of the Law of Unintended Consequences), something which occurs when people misunderstand technology. For example, soot was actually good for stone buildings since it protected them from more aggressive corrosive agents. Clean up the soot in the atmosphere and the stone buildings rot. Advocates of wind farms are thus charged. As Tenner explains, 'Revenge effects come not from using more advanced technology but from accepting deceptive solutions in place of costlier ones. And like other revenge effects, they transform a problem by spreading it in space and time.'

The wind farm argument in Britain, spreading in space and time, is a weak one. Certainly, these islands are the windiest in Europe with an impressive-sounding 'capacity factor' of 27 per cent, but the numerate will immediately see that there is therefore an incapacity factor of more than 70 per cent . . . for 266 days a year the turbines would stand idle. Some of the days it is blowing, the WTGs will have to be shut down against the prospect of dangerous overspeed. This very simply means that even if, or when, Britain's landscape is polluted by the 39,000 WTGs that will be required to meet the 10 per cent 'renewable' energy target, they will still require the near continuous back-up of conventional power stations. That will be the Revenge Effect of wanting energy for nothing.

The special pleading of most environmental groups was succinctly described by Swift:

> All poets and philosophers who find
> Some favourite system to their mind
> In every way to make it fit
> Will force all Nature to submit.

But the fundamental argument against wind farms is one that combines art and technology. Canals are beautiful because they were, at the time, the uncompromised, optimum expression of what was possible. The atrocious electricity pylons which scar Britain were expressions of crassness, greed, waste and ignorance. Alas, despite their elegant sheer white profiles, wind farms have more in common with the wretched old Central Electricity Generating Board's pylons than with Thomas Telford's canals. It's fine to industrialize the countryside, but do it with the best technology . . . not with compromises.

Another example of misunderstood technology is the Toyota Prius hybrid car, presently a bright badge of honour against the satanic forces of carbon. Certainly the Prius is ingenious technologically (as well as a delight to drive), but the real reason it exists is Americans and Japanese are reluctant to buy diesels. Modern diesels are more efficient than petrol-electric hybrids: a recent trans-continental experiment by a US magazine showed a Mercedes-Benz diesel 4x4 was significantly more economical than a comparable Toyota hybrid. Moreover, the complex hybrid technology consumes more resources in manufacturing, is heavy and the batteries present significant disposal problems. And they need to be exchanged after 60,000 miles. The Revenge Effect always operates . . . but then so too does fashion-driven whim, even in areas of activity that you might imagine were subject to the stern laws of science.

The G-Wiz electric car is another example of environmental zealotry failing to understand realities. The G-Wiz is made in conditions of some primitivism and much pollution in Bangalore. If all journeys currently made by petrol-engined cars were done by electrics such as the G-Wiz, some estimates say we would – to replicate the energy requirement – need about 100 more power stations. Probably coal-fired. It is quite easy to demonstrate that a Ferrari 612 Scaglietti is more environmentally responsible than a G-Wiz since its whole life costs are in reality smaller: no one has ever scrapped a Ferrari. People will be scrapping the G-Wiz very soon.

The answer is not only better technology and a better educated awareness of it, but also a change in habits. So far as cars are concerned, don't drive, walk. And develop finer attitudes to all forms of consumption. Litter is a sign of civilization, of prosperity: but that discarded bio-yoghurt pot is one sign we can do without. They knew about litter in ancient Greece. Waste had to be buried in landfill at least a kilometre from Athens's Propylaeum. But just as good technology deplores waste (since heat and smoke and noise are lost forms of energy), good design deplores it too. And by 'design' I do not mean the latest slick offering from a preening Milanese hipster, but a view of the world that is aesthetic.

The unifying principle in all aspects of modern design is a desire to tidy up. Recycling is just the latest aspect of it. Ashes to ashes and dust to dust: recycling adds polyethylene terephthalate to polyethylene terephthalate. Throwing things away is crude and unintelligent. Besides, as the ads say, 'there is no away'. But, again, not all recycling is good. Penny-pinching airlines recycle noxious air in plane cabins to save fuel spent on air-conditioning, leaving us feeling as fresh as dirty laundry after a long flight. And there was the wine connoisseur, astonished at the urological taste of his white Burgundy who said dismissively, 'I think it's been drunk before.' Not everything should always and inevitably be recycled.

But generally recycling is evidence of intelligence at work. The cleverest aspect of the hybrid Toyota Prius is a braking system that captures energy spent in slowing down and uses it to charge the batteries. At the BedZED housing project (Beddington Zero Energy Development) in Surrey, 90 per cent of the horizontal surfaces are impermeable so water can be recovered. In Abu Dhabi Norman Foster is master-planning the world's first zero carbon zero waste community, combining the plan of a traditional pedestrian walled city with photovoltaic power plants and natural energy recovery.

Recycling used to be associated with Third World ingenuity: Persian giveh used old car tyres to make extremely durable shoes. Victor Papanek counselled the world on the philosophy of re-use in his memorable book *Design for the Real World* (1969). But recycling is not just quaint, although the Mozambique model Citroën 2CV sitting near my desk made from a pesticide can has a familiar cute charm. Recycling is one of those disciplines that can inspire genius: already, there are some noteworthy dates in the history of waste management which had their impact on the history of design. The 1875 Public Health Act, for example, required 'movable receptacles' which gave us the ineffable dustbin.

Technology is both a friend and an enemy. There are dates of infamy in this story. 1912, Swiss chemist Jacques Brandenberger creates Cellophane. 1935, Krueger's Cream Ale of Richmond, VA introduces the beer can. Worst of all, 1944, Dow Chemical introduces Styrofoam, only slightly less anti-social than its other signature product . . . napalm. All these things are as unnecessary as Israeli strawberries in December. As Thoreau knew, 'A man is rich in proportion to the number of things he can do without.' But we would not, let us face it, wish to be without high density data storage and signal compression technologies (another way of describing an i-pod).

New technology needs to be used to avoid waste, not create it. Some estimates say we produce 500 kilogrammes of household rubbish per person per annum. New habits need to disavow brainless, undisciplined consumption. The disposable ethic is a thing of the past and a dire embarrassment. Anxiety about the environment is one of the best arguments for good design. Good lives do not have to cost the Earth. Good lives can be made even better by good design. If something is well designed, if something is beautiful, why would you ever want to throw it away? Just compare the Ferrari with the Styrofoam burger box. The Ferrari may be expensive, but it does not cost the Earth.

Nic Marks

A Feeling for Numbers

In 2006, working with my colleagues at nef, we published the Happy Planet Index. At its heart was the design of a new kind of measure to assess how well the nation, or even the world, was doing. It highlights how successful nations are at ensuring good lives for their citizens and how much of the Earth's resources they use in so doing. People often asked how I came up with the idea.

In one sense it is quite an easy question to answer. I just explain how we were writing a report on the links between people's well-being and the environment and I was asked by nef's communications team to come up with some data to illustrate the relationship. So as we had no budgets for primary research I just thought let's calculate how successful nations are at producing long and happy lives for their citizens and divide that by their total resource consumption and *voilà...* – a new indicator is born.

But of course it is not quite that simple and Alain de Botton, the author and philosopher, got it right when he wrote a reflection on the HPI report and said that it '. . . reads like years (decades!) of thought was poured into it'. Well, perhaps nearly right, because it did just sort of happen. Anyway, this reflection is an answer to the question of where the idea came from.

Ever since I was small I have had a feeling for numbers. As a young boy I would play games with numbers. For some reason I had a particular fascination with powers of two. On Saturday mornings I would climb into my parents' bed and start counting with my father 2, 4, 8, 16, 32, 64, 128 . . . I think the challenge was to get one further on in the sequence each week and I can remember struggling with what is two times 16,384! In retrospect it does seem a little odd.

In many ways I wasn't very happy at school. I was sent away to boarding school at the age of eight, and entered a traditional English educational system that at that time was still very hierarchical and didn't respect differences between people. I was, perhaps, an over-sensitive boy, and on the chubby side. I didn't respond well to the teasing that goes on. I would get absolutely enraged about the injustices of school and the meanness of other boys. I certainly, as one teacher put it, 'had a temper'. Now I look back on those times as a 'prickly gift'; it was unpleasant but it gave me a strong sense of injustice and was the start of a deep-felt passion to change 'the system'.

Maths at school became my refuge. Spelling was, and remains, a challenge; art and music weren't really my thing and I could never be bothered learning historical facts. But give me a problem to solve, especially one that involved a definite right or wrong answer, and I was happy.

Before making any real life decisions, I was leaving school and going to Cambridge to read mathematics. Up until this time I had considered myself really very good at maths. I came to the very quick realization that by Cambridge standards I was a very average mathematician. The maths lectures were no better, in fact they were a whole lot worse, as disengaged professors waded through a mass of abstract proofs labelled with a myriad of Greek symbols. To do well in maths at Cambridge you needed to know your betas from your lambdas. There wasn't a whole number in sight!

I floundered around and managed to scrape a poor third in the first-year exams and decided that I had to switch subjects. I explored a few options, even psychology, but didn't pursue it. So instead of maths, I switched to economics. I thought this would be an applied way of using my statistical skills. But I hadn't realized how dismal and annoying economics would be. Lots of questions would start 'if all things are held equal what would happen to x if y increased by 20 per cent' – and I would start my answer with writing 'If all things are held equal (which of course is never the case) . . .' I had one assignment returned with the comment that my essay read more like a manifesto than a reasoned argument – I wish I had kept it.

Half-way through my second year, I got glandular fever and missed most of a term. I had a bad relapse and took it all as a hint that economics, just like maths before it, was not for me. Through some loophole I was able to change subjects for a second time and in my third year I registered to do management studies, which was really applied decision-making, and went on to do a master's degree in 'operational research' (OR). So by a series of somewhat random steps I found my niche – a subject that required you to have a feel for numbers as it was concerned with the useful interpretation of statistics. Over-sophisticated methodologies without good quality data, or that don't address the underlying issue, can only lead to outcomes that are 'precisely wrong', whereas OR is much more interested in being 'roughly right'.

I applied for a job with an American management consultancy firm, and after about two years I began to realize that this meant I wouldn't actually have a life outside work. Then, in the summer of 1989, I went to a talk with my father that changed the course of my working life.

Manfred Max-Neef is a Chilean ecological economist who has been called a 'barefoot economist'. He rejected mainstream development economics and instead proposed a more human-scale development model that put people's real lives at its centre. On that evening he spoke about the incoherence of the dominant economic language and the challenge of ensuring a sustainable future. He went on to suggest that most people spent their lives pursuing issues of secondary importance and didn't notice there were more fundamental questions to be addressed. An example he gave was that many people thought that the world would change for the better if only the people in power changed (probably to be more like themselves) but they never questioned the structure of power itself.

Manfred's ideas struck a chord. That evening gave me a powerful sense of direction, and a new question to ask – how can we create a language to talk about what a sustainable future looks like? It started a train of thought that ultimately led to creation of the Happy Planet Index.

My first significant attempt at addressing this question with numbers was the development with Tim Jackson of the UK's Index of Sustainable Economic Welfare (ISEW). The ISEW was an indicator developed by US economists Herman Daly and Clifford Cobb. The simple idea behind the complex calculations was that current economic measures of progress such as GDP were simply not adequate measures of people's welfare, nor did they assess at all the impacts of human activity on the environment. The structure of the index was a type of macro-level cost-benefit analysis; cashing out the economic and social benefits and then subtracting undesirable social and environmental costs (such as the costs of pollution, long term environmental damage and the effects of inequality).

The work of creating the index was different, with weeks spent in the basement of the London School of Economics, looking for statistics on the incidence of car accidents in the 1950s. Tim and I would meet up in his tiny office near Smithfield's meat market to try to make sense of all the trends and counter-trends. Eventually it started to take shape and the shape told an interesting story. The ISEW had steadily risen from the 1950s, albeit at a slower rate than GDP, up until the mid-1970s but then tailed off. In other words Sustainable Economic Welfare had not increased in the UK since 1976.

In 1994 nef, together with the Stockholm Environment Institute, published the ISEW. What I found interesting was that while many people admitted that they didn't understand the complex calculations behind the index, they would say things like 'that's how it feels', or 'I agree, I don't think life is getting better'. But I knew the index statistically was saying nothing about people's feelings nor indeed anything about their experience of their quality of life, but their reactions to the graphs intrigued me.

While I was doing this work on alternative indicators I started a couple of parallel lives. I did a three-year training in psychotherapy to help me understand people more, and another master's course, in organisational change. I was also working part-time with nef when the then director Ed Mayo said to me: 'Nic, you have been going on for years about how the system is wrong and how this is about measuring the wrong things. Well, I want to set up a programme of work about people's "well-being" and I think you should start it.' So I did. And I decided, in line with Manfred's original advice, to start with a question. We decided that the question should be 'what would policy look like if people's well-being was its aim?'

This meant exploring the new emerging science of well-being. I was heavily influenced by the work of US psychologist Ed Diener, who was the first academic to measure systematically people's subjective well-being, and the Norwegian Joar Vittersø, who persuaded me of the need to understand not only what makes people happy and satisfied but also what interests and excites them. I was also, as a statistician, very impressed by the neatness of the construct of 'Happy Life Years' which was developed as a new metric to use for international comparisons by the Dutch sociologist Ruut

Veenhoven. With this very simple indicator he combines the notions of quality with quantity – by adjusting UN data on life expectancy at birth with people's levels of life satisfaction.

It became apparent to me that here potentially was a way that you could create a new language to talk about a sustainable future. The language of well-being not only resonates with most people – who doesn't want to lead a happy and fulfilled life? – but also had some relevance to Government policy. But perhaps most importantly from the environmental perspective, the language of well-being doesn't rely on an economic model that assumes that more consumption is always better.

In 2004 we launched our 'well-being manifesto'. The manifesto drew attention to the importance of policy in the promotion of good lives for people but it didn't fully address the issue that nothing in life is free and that there is an environmental cost associated with our style of promoting good lives. That idea finally came to me when I was walking our Bernese Mountain Dog up a hill near where we live. I had left my office at home feeling frustrated about not having sufficient funds to do primary research for this project on the environment and people's well-being. I started up the hill and my mind drifted to thinking about many of the good things in my life. When I reached the top I saw the familiar view of the Thames valley stretching out below me, the old Neolithic burial grounds of Wittenham clumps to my right and, interrupting the view, centre stage, the large cooling towers of Didcot power station. Now I have often walked to the top of the hill and considered the power station, where my wife's father used to work, as a cost of our modern way of life. Then somewhere on my way back down the hill I just made the connection that I could divide the well-being benefits of society by its environmental costs – and so the Happy Planet Index came into being.

Well, that's almost the full story. I'm not good at thinking up good names and called my new index the Sustainable Well-being Index (SWI). Then a friend, Jules Peck, said, 'It's got to be called the Happy Planet Index – happy people and happy planet.' So the long answer to the question of how I came to devise a new measure of well-being and sustainability is that it was decades of thought, the influence of many other people, and a couple of moments of inspiration.

6

The Politics of a Good Life

On the fortieth anniversary of a classic speech delivered by Robert Kennedy, in which he famously derided our obsession with economic growth because, 'It measures everything except that which makes life worthwhile', **David Cameron**, the leader of the Conservative Party, returns to the theme. To balance the influence that Gross Domestic Product (GDP) has on political life, he proposes the new measure of General Well-being (GWB). In practice, he argues, this means promoting renewable energy and policies that support family life. He calls for other new indicators to be used, like nef's *Happy Planet Index* which assesses the efficiency with which scarce natural resources are converted into human well-being, measured by relative levels of life expectancy and satisfaction. These, he writes, enable us 'to show that people can live long and happy lives without having to consume the Earth's resources at an inordinate rate'.

Hilary Benn started his job as Secretary of State for Environment, Food and Rural Affairs in the middle of a deluge. His concern about climate change led him to conclude that, just as Britain started the industrial revolution, now it would have to 'lead the world in an environmental revolution'. For him, it's personal too. In Hilary Benn's previous government role in charge of international development he went to Malawi. There he followed in the footsteps of women who walk for hours every day just to collect water. He tried it just once and ended up with neck ache. Climate change is set to make this worse and creates a domino effect. So many hours collecting water means girls have no time left to go to school. Driven by what he saw, he wants Britain to 'lead the world in a low carbon transformation' of the economy. There is a world to win. 'If each country were more able to rely on its own resources for energy,' writes Benn, 'the benefits for peace in the world would be enormous.' He is a man with a plan. 'Where we regulated to protect labour standards through the minimum wage and the social chapter,' he writes, 'now we must regulate to protect the environment.' This will include a new 'green rule' that stops us from borrowing too much carbon or other natural resources from our future. One thing is certain, according to Hilary Benn, 'A good life in the twenty-first century will have to be one that is lived within the earth's means.'

Caroline Lucas has for years been one of Britain's most dynamic members of the European Parliament representing the Green Party. She applauds the new policy focus on well-being rather than economic growth. But she has a problem with the failure to convert concern into real policy and action. Yet, argues Lucas, the politics of sustainability and the politics of well-being go hand in hand. Tackling climate change needs a new economic paradigm that doesn't depend on 'ever increasing resource-based growth'. This fact should be welcomed not feared because such an approach is more likely to improve our well-being too. 'Put simply', she writes, 'the policies we need to live good lives are precisely the policies we need to tackle climate change', but the failure to act risks devastating consequences. According to Lucas, a low carbon world will be safer, with fewer conflicts over dwindling resources. It will also create more jobs as a lower carbon economy requires more hands to make it tick. A society relying on ever-increasing economic growth, however, is more likely to be dissatisfied and unhappy, because the system needs these feelings as emotional fuel to drive endlessly rising consumption. But now, 'as more and more people come to recognize that good lives don't have to cost the Earth', she concludes, 'there is cause for hope.'

David Cameron

In Praise of General Well-Being

The answer to the question 'Do Good Lives Have to Cost the Earth?' is really in the asking: if they *literally* did cost the Earth, they would not actually be much good. Indeed, the very price you have to pay makes it something of a Faustian pact, typifying the kind of human hubris which can only ever lead to doom.

But we should probably not be so literal – 'costing the earth' is a metaphor after all. In this respect, perhaps it is worth fast-forwarding a few centuries from early modern Germany – where the legend of Faustus was formed – to the Kit Kat club in inter-war Berlin. Here, in *Cabaret*, we are told in no uncertain terms that 'Money makes the world go around'. An unabashed celebration of wealth and consumption, the message is simple: good lives do not necessarily have to 'cost the earth', but it certainly helps.

Of course, this is not the case at all. If that were true, why would our society be undergoing the sort of mid-life crisis that is apparent today? For the past few decades we have witnessed unparalleled prosperity. But it is hard to escape the suspicion that there is something not quite right. In some cases, it difficult to put your finger on exactly what it is: a feeling of emptiness, and a lack of defined relationships and solid social structures. In other respects, it is clearly identifiable: rates of drug abuse and depression are rocketing.

It goes to show what most of us instinctively feel: that the pursuit of wealth is no longer – if it ever was – enough to meet people's hope and aspirations; that over-consumption of the world's resources cannot satisfy our most inborn desires; and yes, that quality of life means more than quantity of money.

The questions we now have to answer are: how do we translate this insight into politics? What subjects does it mean we should address? What tools do we have to make sense of it? And ultimately, how can we hope to deliver the higher quality of life – the good lives – we all want to see?

Let me take each of these in turn. First, how can we translate this insight – where quality of life is more important than quantity of money – into politics? To begin with, we need to recognize this insight is nothing new.

Go back some 2,350 years – give or take a few – and Aristotle wrote about what he saw as being the goal of life: achieving 'eudaimonia'. This word has generally been translated as 'happiness' – but not in the sense of how we understand that term today. To most, 'happiness' conjures up the feeling you have during a night out with friends or seeing your football team score the winner in the FA Cup Final. But what Aristotle was describing was not an *emotional* state or disposition, but more a way of life. To him, happiness was about being all that you can – flourishing throughout life with virtues such as courage, pride and friendliness.

Some 2,300 years later – give or take a few – Robert Kennedy brought the idea of personal 'happiness' alive for a modern political audience. In a wonderfully crafted speech given in 1968, he said gross national product

> ... does not allow for the health of our children, the quality of their education, or the joy of their play. It does not include the beauty of our poetry or the strength of our marriages, the intelligence of our public debate or the integrity of our public officials. It measures neither our wit

nor our courage, neither our wisdom nor our learning, neither our compassion nor our devotion to our country; it measures everything, in short, except that which makes life worthwhile.

If reading Aristotle and listening to Robert Kennedy shows us anything, it is that we have to start changing the way we think and talk about politics in this country. It is no longer enough to focus on inputs and outputs, statistics and measurements which seemingly offer quick fix solutions and barometers which politicians love to both obsess and argue about. For the past few decades, the debate has focused intensely on economic arguments. It was necessary – in the 1980s the UK was beset by both high inflation and high unemployment. We needed something to set us back on the path to economic prosperity. Thankfully, we got that.

But as Robert Kennedy eloquently argued, wealth is about so much more than pounds, euros or dollars can ever measure. The spirit of the age today demands social values as well as economic value. This means focusing not just on GDP, but on GWB – General Well-Being. And it also means concentrating on those social, cultural and moral factors that give true meaning to our lives.

This leads to the second question: exactly what subjects does this mean we should address? Well, for one, we need to strengthen families, because no other unit in society does so much to bring up children with the right values, look after our elderly and provide avenues and networks of support to those who need it.

But also central to our well-being is environmental sustainability. I believe, very strongly, that a clean, green environment is absolutely pivotal to our quality of life.

And, as a Conservative, I am in no doubt how important it is that we pass this inheritance on to future generations.

Writing in the late eighteenth century, Edmund Burke, the father of Conservative thought, described history as 'a pact between the dead, the living and the yet unborn'. Put another way, Conservatism is partly about the conservation of the best of our inheritance from our ancestors for the benefit of our descendants: institutions such as parliamentary democracy and common law, for example. And, just as importantly, our collective environment.

Today, everyone understands that this inheritance is in very grave danger. Our generation's reckless disregard for the planet is compromising the ability of future generations to meet their own needs. This is manifested most starkly in climate change, and the more and more unusual and unpredictable weather events devastating livelihoods.

But when I think about climate change and our response to it, I do not think of doom and gloom, costs and sacrifice. I think of a cleaner, greener world for our children to enjoy and inherit. I think of society being able to rise to a whole host of challenges, from our diets to our built environments, with vigour and imagination. And I think of the almost unlimited power of innovation – the new technologies, products and services – and the progress it can bring for our planet and all mankind.

Take solar power. It is providing a well-needed energy source to impoverished communities in rural India and Bangladesh who have no access to national grid supplies. At the moment, many people – mostly young females – are forced to walk for over two days to buy supplies of kerosene to meet their energy needs: an expensive and dirty fuel which can cause death from something very similar to miner's lung (indeed, it has been dubbed 'biomass lung') when used indoors. Solar power provides a cheap and healthier alternative. And by freeing young women from the duty of walking to the nearest urban centres to buy kerosene, areas that have benefited from solar power are witnessing a rise in female education.

Third, what tools do we have at our disposal to make sense of the quality of life agenda? This is perhaps the most difficult question. After all, well-being and quality of life issues are not suited to the kind of statistical analysis that politicians obsess about: we can easily measure our GDP; but what value can we place on the beauty of our surroundings or the quality of our culture?

In terms of environmental sustainability, new measures of progress are emerging. One such example is nef's Happy Planet Index, which uses barometers such as consumption levels and life expectancy to show that people can live long and happy lives without having to consume the Earth's resources at an inordinate rate.

But if we are to make the vital leap from cultural awareness to mainstream action, we must be able to facilitate proper and informed choice. This is where Prince Charles's Accounting for Sustainability project is important, which aims to help businesses, voluntary groups and public sector organizations embed a host of environmental issues in their decision-making processes. This includes a model and methodology to help managers to take greenhouse gas emissions and other sustainability issues into account when making procurement or product design decisions.

The aim is to create a standard environmental balance sheet, just as there is a standard financial balance sheet. This means companies will need to look at stakeholders and not just shareholders. And it also means that consumers will be able genuinely to compare and contrast companies based on their environmental and social performance.

Finally, how best can we hope to deliver a higher quality of life for everyone? I believe that the ideas of the political tradition that I represent, the centre-right, provide the best hope of fulfilling the aspirations of our age. For the centre-left, which treats individuals as units of account, the answer lies in the push of a legislator's pen. For them, a higher quality of life can only be guaranteed and delivered by the state.

On the centre-right, our tradition recognizes that social and cultural change comes from within society rather than without. A tradition that tries to renew and revitalize the relationship between the individual and society, instead of trying to draw a wedge between them. And a tradition where we realize we have responsibilities not just to ourselves, but also a social responsibility to each other. This means governments, businesses, voluntary organisations, local communities, professionals and individuals all playing their part.

So what does this mean for the vital agenda of protecting our environment? To begin with, we must acknowledge that climate change is the greatest market failure the world has ever seen. Greenhouse gas emissions are an externality, affecting the lives of others, with people not paying for the consequences. It is therefore not enough to say leave it to the market: the market has already shown it has failed.

However, we can help make the market work. That is why the greatest responsibility in the fight to save our planet lies with Government, which must give a lead on the issue and set the right framework.

Setting the right framework means creating incentives and removing barriers to remodel the context within which the whole of society makes choices. By creating a price for carbon in our economy, Government can help people make the better choice, inducing individuals and organizations to act in ways that fulfil their wider social responsibilities in the fight against climate change. Businesses assuming their responsibility by pioneering new technologies as well as becoming conscious of their own environmental impact. Local government and community organizations assuming their responsibilities by formulating solutions to combat the environmental damage that blights their neighbourhoods. And ultimately, all of us, as individuals, assuming our responsibility to our collective environment.

That is what social responsibility is all about: it is about society, not the state. It is about saying that the answers to the challenges we face may well be led by politicians, but they will be delivered by people. I think this is the big defining idea for twenty-first century Britain: an idea that has the power to deliver general well-being, because, ultimately, part of what makes life worthwhile is having control over it. And this does not just mean control over your home life, it also means control over your community's life. That is why social responsibility will enhance people's quality of life so much more than the Left's approach of state control: enabling people to be 'do-ers' instead of 'done-fors'; active citizens instead of passive recipients. And far from costing the Earth, fulfilling our responsibilities might just save it.

Hilary Benn

Do Good Lives Have to Cost the Earth?

In the summer of 2007, Britain faced up to the reality of climate change. We experienced the hottest twelve months and the heaviest rainfall on record. Large parts of our country were flooded and thousands of people were left without electricity or clean water from the tap, their homes submerged and their children playing in filthy water. None of us will quickly forget the front page pictures of Tewkesbury, or the images of the main street of Toll Bar under several feet of water.

I started as Secretary of State for Environment, Food and Rural Affairs in the middle of this deluge. And I saw first hand the impact that this unprecedented weather had in some of our most deprived communities.

A few people were angry. But I will always remember the way people worked together, neighbour helping neighbour, collecting and piling sandbags at the doors of elderly people living nearby, and the enormous and selfless effort of so many thousands of people in the emergency services, in voluntary organizations, in local government and in local businesses. In Doncaster, I met a driver delivering sandbags to make sure that families and pensioners were protected, even though the water was rising in his own home. I met staff in temporary rest centres, providing shelter and a comforting word to those who had nowhere else to go. And everywhere I went, I saw people showing the world the humanity and the strength of the British people when times are tough.

These events, and the outbreak of foot-and-mouth disease and of bluetongue that have caused so much hardship for our farming and rural communities, remind us once again that we share a small and fragile planet. The health of each of us, and our families, depends on the health of the world around us: our farmland, our forests, our green spaces, our wildlife and our environment. As the Prime Minister said in his speech to the Labour Party conference, it is 'our shared understanding that our countryside is more than the space that surrounds, it is the oxygen for our towns and cities. And in order to be the country we should be, Britain must protect and cherish not just our cities, but our countryside too.'

More than ten years ago, in this government's first manifesto, we promised to make sure that the environment was at the centre of policy-making and not an optional extra to be added on. We now have cleaner rivers and beaches, purer water to drink, healthier air to breathe, more recycling than ever before and a countryside that is open to each and every one of us to enjoy. But we need to do much, much more.

It is clear to each of us that this century must be a green century, and that Britain can either lead the world in a low carbon transformation of our economy, in protecting our countryside and wildlife, and in renewing our cities, with new jobs in new environmental industries, or we can be left behind. As individuals, we can either learn to live more sustainably today or, in a few years' time, face having to tell our grandchildren why, as a generation, we did not act while we still had time.

Transforming our economy, our cities, our way of life, and cherishing our countryside and wildlife, is something we have to do. But it's not only the pragmatic choice, it's also the right thing to do. Because we now know that climate change is the most serious problem facing the world, that it will kill millions of people, most of them in the developing world, and most of them children who have yet to be born. In fact the World Health Organization estimates that 150,000 people are already dying each year from climate change, enough to fill the Royal Albert Hall thirty-eight times over; millions more will have their lives ruined.

Earlier this year, I visited a village in Malawi, where some local women offered to take me to the water pump. On the way back, I carried a half-full bucket of water and by the end of the fifteen-minute journey, my neck was aching. The women I met do that journey every single day, five times a day. It already takes them hours and for the youngest means they don't have time to go to school and get the education that will help them out of poverty.

Further climate change will mean that thousands like them have to walk further and carry water for longer. It means their daughters won't be able to go to school. It will limit their chances of a better life. And there is nothing they can do about it apart from put their hope in us.

So this is fundamentally about justice, on a global as well as national scale. A good life in the twenty-first century will have to be one that is lived within the earth's means, consuming the resources of just one planet, and not the three that the WWF estimates we are currently using. I am pleased that there is a growing cross-party consensus on the importance of this issue and a commitment to tackling climate change, even if our prescriptions differ. The moral and practical case is too strong for it to be otherwise.

If Britain and the developed world needed less oil, we would be less dependent on the Middle East. If each country were more able to rely on its own resources for energy, the benefits for peace in the world would be enormous. If Britain's air was less polluted, there would be less respiratory disease, our towns would be cleaner and nicer places in which to live, and we could spend more money in the NHS on treating other diseases. And if Britain recycled more, we would need less space for landfill and could use more for social housing and our wildlife.

So, just as we started the industrial revolution, Britain should now lead the world in an environmental revolution, founded on an understanding that in this new century you cannot have social justice and economic growth without environmental sustainability, and that access to a clean and healthy environment, with green space and wildlife, is as much a part of a good life as work, family and friends.

The changes we have to make must be far reaching. Where we have focused on technology and skills to raise labour productivity, now we must adapt our technology and skills to raise resource productivity – the amount we produce from one unit of energy or natural resource. Where we upgraded our skills to respond to a newly globalizing world, we need to help people retrain to work in renewable energy and green technology industries. Where we regulated to protect labour standards through the minimum wage and the social chapter, now we must regulate to protect the environment, from zero carbon homes to renewable electricity generation, from dealing with inefficient appliances to using cleaner cars. Where we forged a new relationship with business, knowing that a strong economy was the best way to achieve full employment and social justice, now we must work with business to create a strong economy that is also a low carbon economy. I am heartened by the action that many of our leading businesses are taking, and am committed to working closely with our small and medium enterprises too in the transition that all of us must make to a low carbon way of living. And where we introduced the 'golden rule' to ensure we did not borrow too much in the public sector, now we must introduce a 'green rule' to ensure we

don't borrow too much carbon or other natural resources
from our future.

Much of this is already happening. Our Climate Change
Bill will make us the first country in the world to put carbon
reduction targets into law. And as the Prime Minister
announced in September 2007, we will now review whether
we need a stronger target than our already ambitious 60 per
cent reduction by 2050.

But people don't see their lives through Bills, and targets,
and plans. They live them, and our politics must be about
their future.

It's not what we have done that really matters now; it is
what we can achieve together for the next generation, reaching out to those who share our values; as individuals, as
activists, as a movement for change. So what could that
change look like?

Imagine a child born today. By the time she is three years
old, we will be recycling and composting 40 per cent of our
waste. By the time she is eight, Britain will be generating 15
per cent of our electricity from renewables – three times as
much as we do now. By the time she celebrates her ninth
birthday, every single new house built that year and for the
rest of her life will be zero carbon, millions of existing
homes will be better insulated, and microgeneration will be
a reality for many of her friends and neighbours, and not
just a few pioneers.

And as she grows up, she will be able to watch the London
Array generating enough electricity from wind power to
supply one in four homes in Greater London. All this is
possible. In fact, this is what we are going to do. But this is
not just about what governments do. Each of us needs to play
our part, and we can see that all over Britain people are
changing the way they live. The carbon calculator (at
www.ActOnCO2.direct.gov.uk; please visit it if you haven't

already!) is helping each of us see how we can change our own lives.

Of course, whatever we do in the UK – and we can do a lot – it is what we do internationally that will in the end determine our chances of victory. At the time of writing, we are looking forward to Bali for what could be the most important meeting of our generation. The world's nations must agree to start negotiations on a new international agreement to replace the Kyoto Protocol, with every country playing its part – from the USA to China. The road to Bali can only lead one way – to a deal, and so over the next few months Britain will be using every source of influence we have to broker that deal.

All of this comes down to politics and the choices we make together. Tackling climate change is not beyond our ability. It simply requires us to decide together that we are prepared to invest in a low carbon future, change the way we travel and consume, do more to protect our countryside and wildlife, and design cities, communities and houses that use less energy while improving our quality of life. We should not pretend that this will not cost money. But just as we have invested to transform our public services for the public good, so too should we make the case for investment in a greener future, just as we should make the case for a firm commitment to internationalism and to Europe as the best way of protecting our environment.

We also need a new kind of politics if we are to succeed. The era of 'Whitehall knows best' is rightly dead and buried. We know that the best solutions come from listening and working with people to help solve their problems and meet their aspirations. We want the government to help us, listen to us, and work alongside us, not to hector us. People rightly want their views and ideas to be taken seriously. And as a Labour politician and constituency MP, I am only too aware that being in Government, lent the power of the state by people based on their trust, is an enormous privilege that demands politicians to listen, and to learn, and to be brave in the decisions we take. Because we're in this together.

Caroline Lucas

The Real Deal?

The happiness industry has never had it so good. In the last twelve months or so, politicians from all three main Westminster parties have theoretically signed up to the idea that the delivery of happiness, and the 'good lives' that go with it, is a core responsibility of Government. Catalysed by the publication in 2004 of Richard Layard's book, *Happiness*, it has become respectable – even fashionable – to be heard publicly talking about it. David Cameron was just the last of many to step into this arena when he last year observed, 'It's time we admitted that there's more to life than money, and it's time we focused not just on GDP but on GWB – General Well-Being.' Happiness indices have sprouted from think tanks and universities, while the Government has set up a Whitehall Well-Being Working Group. Debating happiness, and the role of the state in delivering it, has become a hot political topic.

As someone from a small political party, the Greens, which has been banging on about this agenda for decades, you'd think I'd be pleased. At last politicians appear to be acknowledging that happiness does not depend on endless economic growth and material wealth, but rather on contented families, strong communities, meaningful work, and personal freedom. They are beginning to understand that treating GDP as a useful proxy for well-being can be extraordinarily misleading; and they are therefore groping towards conclusions that good lives – defined as happy and fulfilling ones – don't have to cost the Earth. So far, so good.

The trouble is that the change in rhetoric isn't matched by changes in policy. While Gordon Brown and David Cameron wax lyrical about how improving society's sense of well-being is the central political challenge of our times, their policies are still the same politics of business as usual. Mr Cameron might say that, in order to enable people to have a healthier work/life balance, he wants to create a government that will 'make the British public sector the world leader in progressive employment practices'. When given the chance to do something positive to achieve it, however, he has failed to deliver, twice voting against the Employment Act 2002, which extended paid maternity leave, introduced paid paternity leave, and allowed the parents of young children to request flexible working.

And while Government ministers might accept the proposition that it is *relative,* rather than absolute, wealth which matters most in addressing people's well-being, they have still presided over a period in which policies have continued to widen, not reduce, inequalities.

But nowhere is the gap between the warm words on well-being, and the reality of business as usual, more apparent – or more serious – than in the debate on how to tackle the greatest threat we face, climate change.

Here is the most extraordinary opportunity to bring the politics of well-being to bear on today's greatest political challenge, and yet mainstream politicians are spectacularly failing to do so. Action to address climate change is currently impaled on the hook of economic growth: in other words, politicians dare not advocate the policies so desperately needed genuinely to avert the worst of climate change, because to do so might negatively affect the holy grail of chasing ever-rising levels of economic growth.

Never mind that Nicholas Stern has demonstrated unequivocally that the impact on economic growth of *inaction* is hugely more serious. And never mind, either, that this is the best possible occasion to demonstrate that the politics of sustainability and the politics of well-being go hand in hand: that if policies to address climate change do require a different economic paradigm, one that isn't based on ever increasing resource-based growth, then that's to be welcomed, since such a paradigm might just have a better chance of improving our well-being as well. Put simply, the policies we need to live good lives are precisely the policies we need to tackle climate change.

The failure to grasp this opportunity risks devastating consequences.

Let me explain what I mean. Sir David King, the Government's chief scientific adviser, accepts that in order to keep the rise in global temperatures below 2 °C, we would need to keep greenhouse gas concentrations in the atmosphere at a maximum of 450 parts per million (ppm). However, he has refused to call for a target of less than 550 ppm on the grounds that it would be 'politically unrealistic' – by which he means that it would involve such a dramatic reduction in greenhouse gas emissions that levels of GDP might be affected.

Sir Nicholas Stern echoes him. According to Stern, stabilization at 450 ppm would require global emissions to peak in the next ten years, and then fall by more than 5 per cent per year, reaching 70 per cent below current levels by 2050. 'Stabilization at 450 ppm CO_2 is almost out of reach', Stern says, 'given that we are likely to reach this level within ten years, and that there are real difficulties in making the sharp reductions required with current and foreseeable technologies. Costs rise significantly as mitigation efforts become more ambitious or sudden.'

Since aiming for 450 ppm would cost as much as 3 per cent of world GDP annually to achieve, Stern implies we should aim for between 500 and 550 ppm, a more politically achievable objective, since it would only cost 1 per cent of GDP. And yet, in all probability, this upper target will take the climate beyond the tipping point, with temperatures rising above the 2 °C increase – the increase that Stern makes plain carries 'significant risk' of major environmental collapse, albeit less risk of economic meltdown.

Economic orthodoxy largely dictates that Stern has to reach this conclusion. Business as usual will cost at least 20 per cent of annual world GDP and more, since in terms of climate change, this takes us into unknown territory. The 450 ppm CO_2 stabilization target will cost 3 per cent; 550 ppm, 1 per cent. But that essentially means we're playing a game of Russian roulette, and betting against a scenario which, according to the science, could have a 63–99 per cent probability of tipping us into the worst of climate chaos.

It comes down to this: we can't 'afford' to carry on as we are, because the cost of environmental collapse will be too much. And yet we can't afford the most effective action to prevent this, apparently, because the economic cost will be too much.

The safest option – economically speaking – is to risk a 63–99 per cent chance of environmental collapse, but at the cost of only 1 per cent of GDP. Yet, if we lose, we risk the lives of millions of people, and face a future of ever more devastating famines and floods. No wonder Stern himself calls this 'the greatest and widest ranging market failure ever seen'. Indeed it is the failure of our whole economic paradigm.

It's clear, then, that the failure to apply the politics of well-being to the politics of sustainability could hardly have more serious consequences. How do politicians who acknowledge their responsibility to promote citizens' well-being really imagine that a world of environmental collapse is going to achieve that? If this is where business as usual is taking us, we have no choice but to start unpicking what well-being really means, and start focusing on how to deliver it – rather than remaining fixated on economic growth as an unimaginably flawed proxy.

And this is where we arrive at the fundamental and beautiful concurrence between the sustainability and happiness agendas, which politicians urgently need to wake up to and recognize. Enlightened consideration of what contributes to happiness and well-being points not only to the direct need to protect the environment, but more deeply to the need to move away from endless consumerism and materialism: the very changes which lie at the heart of a more sustainable society.

Put the other way round, a society based on green policies, rather than on endless economic growth, would in fact be likely to be one that resulted in much higher levels of happiness and well-being – because of both the direct and indirect effects of greater environmental protection and stewardship, and the multiple positive direct and indirect social, cultural and spiritual consequences.

In using the terms 'well-being' and 'happiness' interchangeably, I'm aware that I have ignored the literature which equates happiness with pleasure, but attributes to well-being a deeper sense of developing as a person, being fulfilled and contributing to society. Oliver James has summed this up more succinctly than most: 'I regard happiness as chimeric and temporary, akin to pleasure, and I tend to agree with the saying "we were not put on this Earth to be happy"'. And just to underline the point, he adds: 'My focus is on why we are so fucked up, not with dangling a false promise of the possibility of happiness.'

But whether good lives are defined as happy lives or lives of well-being, the bottom line is this: that living a good life and safeguarding the climate are not only simply compatible, they are inextricably connected and mutually dependent. In other words, it serves both our own well-being and the well-being of the planet radically to reform our deeply unsustainable economic system, based on the ever increasing consumption, and waste, of natural resources.

This is the real challenge for Green politicians and campaigners: to emphasize that the changes we need to make to deal with climate change are positive ones, and that the outcomes are desirable in themselves. A low carbon future doesn't have to be a future of shivering around a candle in a cave: it can be a comfortable and more secure one.

It is clear, for example, that the availability of secure and meaningful work is one of the key requirements for a high level of happiness among individuals and societies – and a low carbon world is a highly labour-intensive one. Some jobs would certainly be lost in some of the more carbon-intensive industries, but these would more than be made up for by new jobs in an economy based on repairing, recycling, and re-use. It would also be a world of strong local communities, with greater local production and consumption, and thriving local economies.

A low carbon world would be a much safer world. Current foreign policy in the West is largely based on securing access to fossil fuel resources, often in very unstable parts of the world. If we were more self-sufficient in energy resources, there would be far less chance of resource conflicts.

But crucially, a low carbon world is also likely to be one where we experience greater levels of happiness and well-being. Clearly, in poorer developing countries, a certain quantity and quality of economic growth is urgently needed. But in the richer countries, once our basic needs are met, it seems that more money doesn't make us happier. Beyond a certain point, people's satisfaction with their income depends on its comparability with a norm which is governed by two universal forces in human nature: social comparison, and habituation. Since both of these tendencies are very strong, as Richard Layard puts it, 'it is quite difficult for economic growth to improve our happiness. For as incomes rise, the norm by which income is judged, rises in step.'

Clive Hamilton, in his book *Growth Fetish*, eloquently charts this process in more detail:

> It is . . . vital to the reproduction of the system that individuals are constantly made to feel dissatisfied with what they have. The irony of this should not be missed: while economic growth is said to be the process whereby people's wants are satisfied so that they become happier – and economics is defined as the study of how scarce resources are best used to maximize welfare – in reality, economic growth can be sustained only as long as people remain discontented. Economic growth does not create happiness: unhappiness sustains economic growth. Thus, discontent must be continually fomented if modern consumer capitalism is to survive.

Worse yet, there is a growing body of evidence which suggests that, at the same time that we have become richer, indicators of real mental well-being have been deteriorating. The environmentalist Alan Durning found that, compared to 1950, the average American family now owns twice as many cars, uses twenty-one times as much plastic, and travels twenty-five times further by air. GDP per capita has tripled since 1950 in the USA, and yet satisfaction levels have fallen. More Americans say their marriages are unhappy, their jobs are unfulfilling, and they don't like the place where they live. In the UK, per capita GDP grew 66 per cent between 1973 and 2001, but has failed to translate into higher satisfaction levels. Suicide rates have increased markedly, as have levels of violence, alcoholism, drug addiction and substance abuse.

As Jonathon Porritt starkly concluded, 'The kind of materialism driven on by our contemporary consumer capitalism is leaving people unfulfilled, and is killing the human spirit even as it degrades and despoils the natural world.'

And so, as we face the greatest challenge humanity has yet to confront, the challenge of acting to avoid the worst of climate change, we face an overwhelming question: are we ready for the extraordinary sea change in values, culture and behaviour upon which our well-being – and increasingly our very existence itself – depends? Will we realize fast enough that we cannot avoid environmental disaster except by radically rethinking the social, cultural, economic and political ground rules which govern our lives? Simply put, this implies a repudiation of current neo-liberal economics with its dependence on endless profit and growth, which actually leads to a *reduction* in the overall welfare of people and planet.

As more and more people come to recognize that good lives don't have to cost the Earth, there is cause for hope. The last fifty years have shown us all the things that don't work for human happiness and well-being (principally, what Oliver James calls 'selfish capitalism': ever more growth, privatization, deregulation, and material accumulation). The last few decades have also shown us, with increasing stark-ness, what doesn't work for the planet (principally, burning fossil fuels). The urgent task before us now is to put those two sets of facts together.

7

One Good Life, One Planet: What Does Change Look Like?

Do good lives have to cost the Earth? If you didn't have a view before you picked up this book, there's a good chance that with the range of views on offer you will do so by now. We, of course, think the answer is that they don't. But we also believe that a new set of circumstances is urgently needed for that to be the case. Let's stand back and ask, what kind of public mood and political conditions will allow these ideas to flourish?

Altogether, the arguments in this book make a powerful case for change. But they need to be part of a global case for another way of doing things. The stakes could not be higher. The science of global environmental change shows that our place in our planetary home is very precarious. What kinds of ethical and political arguments can unlock the kind of energy, imagination and commitment that will secure rapid and sweeping change?

This chapter tours the main arguments about global environmental change. It considers their strengths and weaknesses, and makes an optimistic case for our future.

Astronomer Fred Hoyle predicted that an image like the first photograph of the Earth taken from space would 'let loose an idea as powerful as any in history'. It literally shifted our perspective – broadened our horizons – and made us look at our home and ourselves in a new way.

US President Jimmy Carter, considered the most powerful individual on the planet at the time, said that the conservation of natural resources was a mission that represented 'the moral equivalent of war'. In a televised speech on 18 April 1977 he proposed that:

> Our decision about energy will test the character of the American people and the ability of the President and the Congress to govern. This difficult effort will be the 'moral equivalent of war' – except that we will be uniting our efforts to build and not destroy.*

In the 1970s environmental problems seemed to be all about resources. New projections of scarcity, made possible by splicing together economics, ecology and newly available computing powers (farcical and puny by today's standards), energized the debate. Driving it was a conviction that fossil fuels, and oil especially, were not only polluting, but would become increasingly expensive and difficult to find. Although right in principle, their relatively primitive monitoring and computing powers meant that their time scales were off. The result was that people felt environmentalists were 'crying wolf'.

This planetary politics is still young. Just three decades separate us from Carter's carefully chosen phrase. Scientific and policy leaders have returned to martial analogies as they

*http://www.pbs.org/wgbh/amex/carter/filmmore/ps_energy.html

work to recruit broad public support for a de-carbonized economy. Al Gore closes his presentation and film *An Inconvenient Truth* with a reference to the focused national effort of Second World War economies allied with the potential for dramatic economic, technological and social change.

Following directly in the footsteps of former UN weapons inspector Hans Blix, and the prominent climate scientist Sir John Houghton, the British Government's Chief Scientific Advisor David King referred to climate change in 2004 as 'a greater threat than terrorism', and former Prime Minister Tony Blair has described the fight against climate change as akin to the battle against fascism and the Cold War.

Such comparisons with wartime struggle are powerful. These are collective calls to action that draw upon a powerful stock of references that touch on the integrity of a nation state and bundle them together with deep-seated emotions linked to personal security, identity and a way of life. At the same time they justify the reach of Government into the workings of the market and households. This is a call for politicians to get their hands on the big levers again.

Given that, by growing consensus, we may have as little as five to ten years to stabilize global concentrations of greenhouse gases before irreversible climate change effects kick in, it's worth asking under what circumstances the scale of necessary change has happened before.

Have we ever, under any circumstances, re-engineered the economy to the degree now necessary, reducing consumption, and in so short a time? This is where the war analogy is appropriate, and the answer is yes. It involved the public sector aggressively leading the wider population in wholesale lifestyle change.

Culturally and politically, things are very different today, but we can take some comfort from the knowledge that between 1938 and 1944, in the face of a very different threat, we achieved remarkable things. People also forget that the population didn't just fall in behind the war effort, many needed convincing of the necessity to act. The Government was compelled to publish *Data for the Doubtful* to help convince a dubious population. There is perhaps an echo of today's continuing debate with 'carbon appeasers'.

The gradual introduction of luxury taxes and schemes to promote war savings was a huge struggle, constantly agonized over. The Government employed the best creative artists of the day to persuade people. But it worked. Together with rationing, over that six-year period there was a 95 per cent drop in the use of motor vehicles, use of household electrical appliances dropped 82 per cent and consumption of all goods and services fell by 16 per cent, and much higher at household level. There were surprising benefits too.

People spent more of their disposable income on 'amusements', and, unsurprisingly, public transport. Staggeringly, a nation consuming less, but better, saw infant mortality drop by nearly a quarter in the same period. Perhaps the strongest analogy is to do with the scale and speed of necessary change.

Of course, people in the UK will not yet be ready for a 'war economy' model of action on climate change. Climate change is a more diffuse and hidden enemy. Fascism presented a tangible threat to specific and bounded communities.

NASA's image of the Earth at night from space helps us to see that the prime driver of climate change is an incredibly active economic system – fossil fuel-powered capitalism. And it is virulent. The threat of climate change is generated not by projections of scarcity as in the 1970s, but by an aggregation of individual choices that result in uncertain and dispersed, but major global risks.

Who is responsible for these risks and how do we point fingers? The historic emissions of rich countries and their typically very high levels of emissions per person, invite them to confess and display leadership. To soothe our guilt and reduce our responsibility, it is becoming commonplace to conjure China or India as a new class of perpetrator. But, in fact, this refers only to these countries' relatively small, emergent middle classes who are copying our carbon-intensive lifestyles: the dishwasher, the car, the trip to Venice.

The complex new mappings of responsibility suggest that if this is the 'moral equivalent of war', if we wish to locate the enemy we must raise a mirror and look into it.

Other comparisons will also be needed to make sense of this moment. These share the broad historical, political or economic scope of Carter's, Gore's and Blair's 'equivalent of war' argument. Can they help us to feel that we can achieve good lives that don't have to cost the Earth?

Sooner or later, most campaigns that tackle social justice get compared to the abolition of slavery. The connection to climate change is that, following the well-rehearsed media routines of reporting global poverty, the vulnerable are seen in stories about flood and drought victims. This helps to lift the statistical predictions of harm off the pages of scientific reports and give them a life in our political imagination. It is one of the few ways that the voiceless get represented, though imperfectly, in political debates. In this way the poor of desertifying rural China and the flood-threatened inhabitants of the Ganges delta become the 'poster children' of climate change.

Environmental and more recently anti-poverty campaigners have been effective in a world in which good media advocacy can resemble a proxy for democratic representation. These appeals to consider the fates of fellow humans – distant from us in space or time – parallel appeals for the abolition of slavery. They combine peerless moral authority and hint at the promise of success.

However, there are hazards with the use of 'victimhood'. It can foreshorten the need to give the vulnerable their own voice in the climate change debate. One of the most powerful weapons of the original abolitionists was the self-penned life stories of the slaves and former slaves themselves.

An image or scripting of a victim deployed within an argument for emissions reductions is a device and not a form of representation. At the very least people living on the front line of climate change need to be allowed their own voice rather than having a script written for them.

If the vulnerable of northern China or the Ganges delta then say that they are more interested in adapting to climate change by, for example, migrating, or by copying the rich world's middle class model of fossil-fuelled comfort, that will be merely the chickens of our own mistakes coming home to roost.

On the same grand historical scale, many have promised that a second industrial revolution – a solar century – is dawning. They argue that it can radically reduce carbon emissions and deliver a novel route to wealth creation.

But even this path is not straightforward. The global economy is full of obstacles. Illiberal rules prevent the easy spread of technology, and history tells us that it is nearly always better to grow solutions at the local level, where everyone can benefit, than to parachute in ready-made solutions.

The appeal of this argument for its proponents is that it responds to both threat and opportunity. The threat here is not to vulnerable people, but to vulnerable supply chains, financial institutions, markets or shifting tax and regulatory regimes. The opportunities, expressed in the breathless confidence of an unshakably secure economic political system, are captured in phrases such as 'win-win solutions' and 'achieving the triple bottom line' (a reference to combined economic, social and environmental objectives).

Responding to climate change opens up new markets for new products, and creates a new commodity market for carbon in the world of tradable permits designed to reduce emissions. This promise of a second industrial revolution is compelling: clean wealth creation – distributed at speed across a global economy. The power to shape market prices in a commodity such as carbon, and send signals throughout an economic system, holds enormous potential to re-engineer the way we approach many of our daily choices. Set within environmental limits and tempered by social objectives, markets can play an important role in making progress towards 'good lives'.

But many have pulled apart these attempts to commodify carbon and bind it into the profit-investment-profit cycle. They show that unintended and perverse outcomes are always possible. When the European emissions trading scheme was set up, for example, badly designed ground rules rendered it ineffective and potentially damaging to the cause of controlling global warming.

There's also the danger of fast-growing, big, bad monocultural 'Kyoto forests' blanketing the landscape, regardless of their economic and environmental consequences or impact on local communities, or, as mentioned in the introduction, the spread of palm oil plantations appearing in place of old growth forest.

Some climate-related mechanisms may present new ways of embedding or even extending exploitation. The so-called Clean Development Mechanism, a part of the international climate agreement, is meant to be part of accelerating the move to low carbon economies. But the thinking behind such measures is generated a long way upstream from democratic processes and grassroots experience. For markets to work to deliver lasting carbon emission reductions they will have to be structured in ways that represent a global and democratic decision, and draw on the wisdom of local experience.

Furthermore, without some element of global distribution of the benefits of economic development – however clean and bright – the second industrial revolution will be seen to be a private party attended by the (already) rich. Those parties, numbering in their billions, that are most threatened by climate change, and already most excluded from the economic system that generated the problem, will not simply sit to wait out the floods and sandstorms.

Still others argue that action on climate change represents the political equivalent not of war, but of defence spending. In this argument pump-priming investment by the state in 'problem solving' (i.e. war-winning) technologies will have multiple benefits.

Technology plays a part in almost all responses to climate change, but there is a particularly influential body of opinion that sees it as sufficient in itself. This argument proposes technology-forcing on a scale parallel to the investment during the Cold War that created the so-called military-industrial complex. The motives behind this argument are threefold. The first is shared with most of the other positions outlined here, and centres on the mitigation of emissions. There is a parallel with the commitment to spend a certain portion of the national wealth on the preservation of the integrity of its borders. Climate change has from very early on been framed as a security issue in some key quarters: NATO staff college conferences were pondering these dimensions even before the 1992 Rio Earth Summit. The second motive is the desire for a potentially highly profitable new industrial sector that can compete on a global scale. The third is the promise of increasing energy independence – again motivated by concern specifically for national security.

The framing of the issue in the national interest may help to draw in new support for action. However, presenting technology as something that happens in a parallel world, separate from markets, taxes, and politics is a naïve simplification of the complex way that new products and processes make their way into the world. The thwarted potential of renewable energy provides one, in fact several, examples. Combining a range of new and proven ancient technologies, renewable energy is still the poor relation in the energy mix, in spite of being clean, inexhaustible and an efficient investment in both cost and energy terms. There are many reasons: lack of support, the wrong price and regulatory structure, and a power system not designed to benefit from or encourage the major renewable energy sources. There is also the small matter of them having been briefed against over many years by competing sectors like the nuclear industry.

The notion of insurance, perhaps, gives us a more robust metaphor. The insurance industry developed as a means of managing risks and spreading costs across a community – whether a community of traders acknowledging the risk to their livelihoods of their cargoes at sea, or some years later, of householders sharing the costs of protection from the risks of fire damage to their homes.

The metaphor works harder than simply suggesting the spread of risks within a community. Most forms of insurance reward policy-holders who are prepared to reduce risks by adapting their behaviour – for example, fitting better window and door locks, or driving smaller, cheaper, less powerful cars. A reduction in collective costs is then rewarded with reduced premiums. This comparison with insurance will help to explain to people why certain costs must go up, why some forms of adaptation must be invested in and why some practices must change.

This is, in fact, more than a metaphor. Increased insurance premiums generated by climate impacts such as floods, storms and subsidence are already the first direct instance of climate change reaching into the paperwork of millions of boardrooms and kitchen tables around the world. One of the powerful things about this reference to insurance is that it neatly connects individual and collective risks, and shows a way of spreading costs. But the comparison only makes sense if the 'insurance cover for climate change' is universal.

The last comparison in our whirlwind tour is with the development of welfare states in mid-twentieth century Europe. An improbable coalition gathered in the 1930s and 1940s around the idea that capitalist societies needed to strike a new deal between business, Government, workers and the wider society.

Rather than striking or starting revolutions, many in the working class supported a capitalist society that guaranteed them secure work, improving wages and relative comfort in old age. Business accepted that they needed to invest in the health and education of their workforce in order to be internationally competitive (and to insulate against revolution). The state's role was to oil the wheels of this new hybrid machine. Although the 'rolling back of the state' during the 1980s clouds many memories, it is important to recognize how startlingly successful this approach proved to be in the post-war reconstruction of Europe.

The fact that it was not driven by one body of interests or set of arguments, but resulted from an alignment between previously competing forces made it politically robust across several decades. It resulted in dramatic advances in education, health and life chances in the populace.

We are not trying to invoke a revival of a welfare state world repainted with a deep green tinge. The point is that there are features of that deal that resemble a deal that we can – must – make now. This deal is one where the global community might be made both secure and economically vital. The moment we are living through demands a robust coalition of the concerned citizen, the community, the entrepreneur, the NGO that will speak up for the vulnerable, and the civil servant that will weed and tend the new partnerships. The most important seat at the table, and the one that has been left empty the longest, is for the democratically elected politician who will show compelling leadership.

This reference to the welfare state isn't actually a separate comparison but a weaving together of points from all of the above. The moral equivalent of war? Yes – this is a moment as urgent and radical as wartime: we should be marshalling our resources to 'secure our global climate borders'. The ethical parallel of the abolition of slavery? Certainly our increasing awareness that our polluting ways have awful consequences for distant others are forcing us to extend the boundaries of our ethical community.

A second industrial revolution? There is no doubt that the world's first solar billionaire – a Chinese entrepreneur – is bringing together the same mix of technology, timing, investment and daring, with consequences just as far-reaching as those of the first industrialists. The political equivalent of defence spending? It is true that in building a broad coalition of support for a transition away from an unsustainable economy it will be important to demonstrate the benefits in terms of security and jobs that will accrue to nations that pursue a sustainable path. Green taxes similar to paying an insurance premium? This is an intuitive way of explaining why and how we need to spread risks (and generate funds to cope with adapting to change) across our now global society.

The reason we conclude with the comparison with the welfare state is that there was one group of actors who were essential to its success. Business, workers and the wider society were all looking for a new way forward – but they required the leadership, imagination and patient brokering of politicians to make a new moment, to frame a new direction.

The societies that formed welfare states were not unified in their interests and ambitions for the future – far from it. But they came to a deal about what the most robust next steps should be, and the deal rewarded everyone.

Achieving a good life for more than 6 billion people, without further threatening the ecological systems on which we all depend, is the greatest challenge of our age. Yet this statement – made many times by many people – easily looks dead on the page. What the authors in this book have shown is that there are so many ways in which our dominant measures of personal and economic success are incomplete – and often perverse. Taking a fresh look at the world, we can see that good lives don't need to cost the Earth – indeed they offer our best chance of preserving it. This realization needs to become the central political idea of our time.

Joe Smith and Andrew Simms

Extras

1 A Day in the Life of the Good Life

Imagining what it might be like. Coming soon to a street near you . . .

On waking

With less time spent working the choice is yours – lie in, go for a run, read a novel – no, write a novel. Having rediscovered the real meaning of a good life, previously over-consuming rich countries have now cured most cases of work addiction. In this 'downshifted' world the phrase 'rush hour' has become a half-remembered documentary curio. More flexible working practices have made it much easier for people to work part-time, take sabbaticals and tailor where and when they work. Our society has begun to get the hang of how computing and IT can make for smart work, rather than generate slave work. Those choosing the early morning run enjoy fresh air in their lungs and clear paths as dramatic reductions in traffic have transformed city air and streets. People in love with their pillow or partner can linger in bed – they'll hear more bird-song and less traffic.

Breakfast

No need to sweat over every shopping decision: business and Government have got it together to make socially and environmentally sustainable trade the (carefully checked) norm. The weekly food bill has gone up – but so has the quality, and we're saving lots of money later in the day (see below). The damaging consequences of cheap food systems have gradually been rolled back. Coffee, cereal, milk, fruit: these have returned to their historic role of simple pleasures, unsullied by association with distant exploitation or polluted local rivers. This is sustainable consumption universalized – no more scanning labels. A few deft moves in boardrooms and Parliamentary chambers helped to make food markets fair and sustainable.

For an international meeting – step on to your balcony: video-conferencing and networking software is so slick and intuitive that you have massively reduced your need to travel for work. The hours gained, backache cured and wrinkles postponed make you more effective and committed to the work you do. But these changes are about more than work. Social networking software has thrown you together with new people where you live – your desktop gives you a global network, but also connects you in new – live – human ways to the community where you actually live.

For those happy to live without a computer there are plenty of benefits in the new sense of community that has evolved from the revival of real local shops (where the shopkeepers actually remember who you are) and the way that residential streets and town centres, liberated from suffocating traffic, have become people-friendly. Streets are safer for children to play in, with some entirely car-free, and many towns have reclaimed central plots of land as public squares. A calmer environment and more opportunities for casual contact between neighbours means people gather and talk to each other more and, as a result, even in cities people, and especially the elderly, feel less lonely.

Take some time out late morning to plan your long awaited summer trip. While the big increases in the cost of fossil fuels has seen international travel become a much rarer experience, it tends to be much better – and longer – when you do head off on your travels. In the bad old days you might have dashed off a postcard after thirty-six hours in a congested foreign capital while you waited in an airport queue. These days it will be more a matter of picking out a few choice photos from the hundreds you'll take on your once in a lifetime (yes, once) three-month trip to India. Travel returns to being a pleasure and an adventure. With more leisure time and good cycle and public transport links, low impact local excursions are a much-loved part of many people's lives. But with our experience of both cities and countryside transformed by investment in really great public spaces – whether it's the park or local recreation ground, the village hall, local pub or café, theatre or cinema – people feel less need to get away in order to unwind.

Lunch

Need to get out of the house? Take a short stroll to one of the thousands of courtyard and street cafés that are enjoying the cleaner air and quieter streets. Plenty of these are cheap workplace and school cafés that have opened their doors to locals. The combination of a few familiar faces, a random mix of new ones, and a daily changing menu of fresh local food bought and cooked with a close eye on the long chain of environmental consequences makes food a daily pleasure. You sit outside at a table in the hot spring day and allow yourself a private thought: 'I know there are more losers than winners with climate change, but just for a few minutes let me enjoy the moment.'

Afternoon

A journey to work? Problems are as big as you make them: it used to be said that people wouldn't give up their cars. Cars were bought; roads were built; resources (including our own wallets) were burnt in pursuit of a very particular form of mobility that becomes less enjoyable and more polluting the more people take it up. But instead of denying people their cars (and the liberty, safety, reliability and, for some, status, they offered) the big breakthroughs were made by offering people really appealing alternatives. Some of these were alternatives to travel (like the conferencing tools). But we all want to move about. So, by raising revenue from polluting and inefficient fossil fuel-run cars governments were able to completely transform people's experience of cities and towns. Owning and driving cars to meet most of your mobility needs has come to seem simply eccentric. Lifespan and quality of life have dramatically increased as a result of cities being redesigned around people – and walking and cycling – not cars. Transport options range from trains, trams and quiet clean buses, to on-demand rural shared taxis and simple car-share schemes that meet the range of needs we have through a year. The common 'ting' of the cycle bell is as much to say 'hello', as to remind you that you're stepping across a cycle path. And when we do get in a car, the uncongested roads and beautifully designed hyper-efficient vehicles remind us what a great invention these things can be.

Afternoon at the coal face? Perhaps your office is one of the last bits of the building to have a green makeover. In the hot spring weather you've got to turn the air-conditioning on. It is not as wasteful as the old machines, but you know that some of the electricity is still going to be fossil fuelled. It's not a solution for the long term, but you can comfort yourself with the knowledge that the increased costs brought about by carbon taxes have got your finance department talking to your estate department who are talking to the builders about natural ventilation systems. In the meantime the tax raised is salving all of your consciences. In an idle moment you reflect on where this cash goes, and why that matters. One of a series of breakthrough climate deals between north and south ensures that the inhabitants of Brazil, especially those living in the Amazon, are directly rewarded for their stewardship of the ecological services that the rainforest provides to the whole planet. As we descend gradually from our carbon-fix high we can at least ensure that our habit is funding some security for us all by protecting these key carbon sinks. The bill for your air-conditioning that helps you cope with climate change in your office is in effect helping to pay the bill to keep the global air-conditioning running in the Amazon basin.

Playtime

You don't have to think too hard about it, but these connections between near and far are cropping up in all corners of life.

Dinner

Time released from long working days, and the fact that fast food and ready meals have gone up in price now that they reflect their full ecological costs, has seen a revival of home cooking. With lots more single households there are some twists. More people get together to take turns to share informal meals in a neighbourhood. There are delivery services providing decent food in returnable containers for people without either enough time or inclination for the kitchen or company.

Evening

Stories and music are as old as campfires. For a time we forgot it, but being actively involved in making entertainment made us feel much better than just passively watching others perform. One of the first things taught in school now is the medical evidence that watching TV induces a mental state almost identical to clinical depression. Perversely, though, the fashion for reality TV talent shows early in the twenty-first century triggered a widespread revival in people wanting to do things for themselves so, in any case, we started to spend fewer and fewer hours trancelike in front of the television. It's now common in pubs, clubs and in any available hall to find groups of friends showing films made by themselves on cheap, easy to use equipment, and putting on a wide range of music and other performances. People are intrigued and drawn in by the fact that they can actually get to know the musicians and film-makers, because they are likely to live in the area.

Just as people are happier to go out more locally during the day, because towns have become more pleasant places to be, the same is true at night. As in countries like Italy, in the early evening people of all ages take to strolling around town, just for the sake of it. The increase in spare time means people start reviving half-forgotten festivals and celebrations, as well as creating new ones to mark everything from important global events, to the seasons, local history, people and impor-tant events. There is much more partying in general.

A revival of distinctive local economies also brings more character back to different areas, making it worth travelling around the local area to visit other unique local festivals, bars, restaurants, cinemas and theatres. Clone towns dominated by identical chain stores and outlets are consigned to history, as are the embarrassing fashion crimes of hugely flared trousers, big perms and jackets with padded shoulders.

The good life is active, but it's full in a good way. By press-ing all the right buttons it creates its own energy to thrive. So, by the time evening turns to night, most people are still in the mood to press other right buttons on the one they love. Then we'll settle, tired maybe, satisfied surely, to take stock of how things have gone, round off our day, look forward to the next one and enjoy our sleep, deeply.

2 Action Plans

A Global Ten Point Plan for Good Lives that Don't Cost the Earth*

1.Eradicate extreme poverty and hunger

Increasing material wealth in (so-called) developed countries does not lead to greater happiness, and extreme poverty systematically undermines people's opportunities to build good lives for themselves and their families. We urgently need to redesign our global systems to distribute more equitably the things people rely on for their day-to-day livelihoods, for example income, and access to land, food and other resources.

2. Improve healthcare

High life expectancy in a country reflects good healthcare and living conditions, and has a positive influence on people's sense of well-being. Globally we need to increase access to clean water, halt the rise in diseases such as HIV/AIDS and malaria, and reduce child and maternal mortality. The World Health Organization estimates that everyone in the world could be provided with a good level of basic healthcare for just $43 per person per year.

3. Relieve debt

Many developing countries are forced to prioritize the service of crippling financial debt over providing a basic standard of living. Debt sustainability calculations should be based on the amount of revenue that a government can be expected to raise, without increasing poverty or compromising future development.

4. Shift values

Value systems that emphasize individualism and material consumption are detrimental to well-being, whereas those that promote social interaction and a sense of relatedness are profoundly positive. Governments should provide more support for local community initiatives, sports teams, arts projects and so on, while acting to discourage the development of materialist values where possible (for example, by banning advertising directed at children).

5. Support meaningful lives

Governments should recognize the contribution of individuals to economic, social, cultural and civic life, and value unpaid activity. Employers should be encouraged to enable their employees to work flexibly, allowing them to develop full lives outside the workplace and make time to undertake voluntary work. They should also strive to provide challenges and opportunities for personal development at work.

6. Empower people and promote good governance

A sense of autonomy is important at all levels for people to thrive, and there is growing evidence that engaging citizens in democratic processes leads to both a more vibrant society and happier citizens. Promoting open and effective governance nationally and internationally, including the peaceful resolution of conflicts and elimination of systematic corruption, is important for all of us in achieving greater well-being in the long term.

7. Identify environmental limits and design economic policy to work within them

The ecological footprint gives us a measure of the Earth's biocapacity that, if over-stretched, leads to long term environmental degradation. Globally we need to live within our environmental means. One-planet living should become an official target of Government policy with a pathway and timetable to achieve it. The UK currently consumes at just over three times this level. If everyone in the world consumed as we do in the UK, we would need 3.1 planets like Earth to support us.

8. Design systems for sustainable consumption and production

We need to reverse the loss of environmental resources, conserve our ecosystems and integrate a sustainable development approach throughout the global community. Ecological taxation can be used to make the price of goods include their full environmental cost, and to encourage behavioural change. Clear consistent labelling that warns of the consequences of consumption, as with tobacco, would also help, as well as giving manufacturers full life-cycle responsibility for what they produce.

9. Tackle climate change

For the UK to play its part in preventing catastrophic and irreversible global warming it is estimated that we will need to cut our greenhouse gas emissions by at least 3 per cent every year. More broadly, rich countries need to meet and exceed their targets for reducing greenhouse gas emissions set under the Kyoto Protocol, cutting emissions to a level commensurate with halting global warming so that temperature rise is kept well below 2 °C. After 2012, and in subsequent commitment periods of the Kyoto Protocol, emissions cuts should put industrialized countries on track to savings of up to 80 per cent by 2050.

10. Measure what matters

People all over the world want to lead happy and complete lives, but we all share just one planet to live on. We urgently need our political organizations to embrace and apply new measures of progress, such as the HPI and adjusted GDP indicators. Only then will we be equipped to address the twin challenges of delivering well-being for all while remaining within genuine environmental limits.

*Taken from *The (un)Happy Planet Index*, nef (the new economics foundation), London, 2006

A Personal Ten Point Plan for Good Lives that Don't Cost the Earth

1. Take a walk
Living well is a walk in the park, really. Not only will you get a buzz from the exercise and a longer term health benefit if you do it regularly, you'll reap psychological benefits from spending time outside in green space.

2. Enjoy the finer things
Set some time aside to browse your local market for really good ingredients; it's cheaper than the supermarket, and more fun. Get creative in the kitchen and if you're not too confident, grab your favourite celebrity chef's cookbook. Then share the fruits of your labour. Nothing beats a glass of wine and a good meal with friends.

3. Have less, do more
We always think that the next must-have gadget or fashion item will make us happier, but our brains play funny tricks, making us gradually more dissatisfied with our possessions, leaving us always hankering for more and more (psychologists call this 'adaptation'). In reality, most people would be happier if they spent more time doing enjoyable things with their families and friends, even if this meant earning a bit less

money and focusing a bit less on the next purchase. The city of Sao Paulo in Brazil banned outdoor advertising as 'visual pollution'. Other cities could well follow this example to help remove the constant pressure to consume. So, time to get off the treadmill . . .

4. Time is not money

It's much more valuable. Nobody's final words were, 'I wish I'd spent more time at the office.' Spend a few weeks keeping a diary of how you spent your time and then think about whether you really got the most out of it.

5. Think positively about the future and make plans

People who have clear life goals and are able to work towards them by engaging in enjoyable activities – such as setting up a club, a community project or a website about one of their passions, learning to dance or play an instrument, planning expeditions, editing a magazine or writing a book – tend to have higher levels of well-being than people who 'languish'. Working towards a long term goal is always more satisfying than the short term reward from a 'quick fix' like going shopping.

6. Reduce, Re-use, Repair and Recycle

This mantra about how to manage waste can be applied to all the materialistic aspects of our lives. The reward of finding hidden treasures in a charity or second-hand shop, and bringing them back to life is far greater than buying and assembling a cheap flat-pack piece of furniture or throw-away fashion item. When you do buy new stuff buy for the long term: aim for beautifully designed things that will last well. It will save you money in the end. Challenge yourself to one small bag of waste a week. Compost, or if you live in a small space, invest in a wormery. Your new friends will be delighted to help you recover nutrient-rich compost from your kitchen scraps which you can then use in your garden.

7. Cut your use of dirty energy
Buy green energy or make your own with a range of renewable devices. Think of the satisfaction of knowing that your own home can sell energy back to the national grid, and consider how this will also protect you from rising energy prices. Start with an energy audit of your home, and get one of those clever monitoring gadgets that reveal your real-time energy use. Then you can gawp at how much energy boiling a kettle uses. You'll soon see where you can cut back. Switching to a green electricity supplier means you are voting with your plugs.

8. Live authentically
Demand authenticity, seek out things with character and individuality that are connected to a person or a particular place. As far as possible, avoid bland, identikit, corporately branded goods, and turn the tide on the clone towns created by having too many chain stores, where every high street ends up looking the same. By doing so, you will help support a more vibrant and thriving community in your local area.

9. Get creative
Make music, make art, play games, make your own performances with friends and rediscover your creative side. It's not only meditative, it develops self awareness.

10. Eat well
Humans were never supposed to eat vast quantities of meat. From the mid-1950s to 1978, our consumption of meat in rich countries went up by nearly 50 per cent per person. But

nutrition derived from meat is extremely inefficient. It takes hundreds of litres of water to produce one litre of milk, and around one-fifth of greenhouse gas emissions are from live-stock farming, the result of both deforestation and the flatu-lence of cows. A less meat-based diet will significantly reduce your ecological footprint. *And buy organic, locally grown produce:* Organic farming methods are far less energy and chemical intensive, and more environmentally friendly. Buying food grown more locally also cuts energy used in transport. Join a 'box scheme' and rediscover indigenous seasonal fruit and vegetables.

3 Where to Find Out More

The Groups behind this Book

Do Good Lives Have to Cost the Earth? grew out of The Interdependence Day project, a partnership between nef, the Open University and others.

The Interdependence Day Project: Making New Maps for an Island Planet

What is it? Who is it? And why is it happening? The Interdependence Day Project aims to find new ways to respond to the fact of an interdependent world. It includes a mix of research, events, publications and new creative work, all grown from collaborations between researchers, the public, academics, artists, campaign groups and the media. Interdependence Day is a joint venture between organizations and individuals committed to a better public understanding of the fate of the planet, and the people with whom we share it.

Demands to save the planet from environmental catastrophe, or to act on poverty are often daunting in scale and
distant from daily life. But there is good news. In a globalized
world, the interdependence of all living things grows clearer
by the day. And, all over the world, people are responding to a
growing awareness of their interdependence in a variety of
creative and innovative ways. The Interdependence Day
Project is about refreshing debates about the policies, choices,
actions and technologies that promise to change our world
for the better.

For more information see: www.interdependenceday.co.uk.

nef (the new economics foundation)
nef
3 Jonathan Street
London
SE11 5NH
020 7820 6300
www.neweconomics.org

nef is the UK's leading independent 'think-and-do-tank'.
Founded in 1984, it aims to improve quality of life by promoting real economic well-being. nef develops inno-vative solutions that challenge mainstream thinking on economic,
environmental and social issues. It works in partnership,
putting people and the planet first. It produces cutting edge
research and campaigns on issues ranging from climate
change to well-being, and the spread of clone towns. It established the Centre for Well-Being in 2006, to study and
advance its understanding. The Centre researches the measurement of well-being and other factors that influence it, and
also provides training and analytical tools for others to be able
to assess and positively influence well-being.

The Open University
Department of Geography
Faculty of Social Sciences
The Open University
Walton Hall
Milton Keynes
MK7 6AA
01908 654456 or 654472
http://www.open.ac.uk/socialsciences/about-the-faculty/
departments/geography/

The Open University (OU) is the United Kingdom's only university dedicated to distance learning. With most courses no previous qualifications are required to study and there are around 150,000 undergraduate and more than 30,000 post-graduate students. It is ranked among the top UK universities for the quality of its teaching. The geography department at the OU has a record of producing innovative research and teaching in both human and environmental geography.

Further Reading

Beyond Growth, Herman E. Daly, Beacon Press, 1996.

The Consolations of Philosophy, Alain de Botton, Hamish Hamilton, 2000.

Dancing in the Streets: A History of Collective Joy, Barbara Ehrenreich, Granta, 2007.

The End of Over-consumption Marius de Geus, International Books, 2003.

England in Particular: A Celebration of the Commonplace, the Local, the Vernacular and the Distinctive, Sue Clifford and Angela King, Hodder & Stoughton, 2006.

Happiness & Economics, Bruno S. Frey and Alois Stutzer, Princeton University Press, 2002.

Happiness: Lessons from a New Science, Richard Layard, Penguin, 2006

The High Price of Materialism, Tim Kasser, The MIT Press, 2002.

The Loss of Happiness in Market Democracies, Robert E. Lane, Yale University Press, 2000.

Manufacturing Discontent: The Trap of Materialism in Corporate Society, Michael Perelman, Pluto Books, 2005.

Not Buying It: My Year without Shopping, Judith Levine, Pocket Books, 2007.

The Paradox of Choice: Why More is Less, Barry Schwartz, CCCO Harper Collins, 2004.

Stumbling on Happiness, Daniel Gilbert, Harper Perennial, 2007.

The Theory of the Leisure Classes, Thorstein Veblen, George, Allen & Unwin, 1899.

Useful Websites

www.adbusters.org – adbusters describes itself as 'a global network of artists, activists, writers, pranksters, students, educators and entrepreneurs' and helps to organize international 'buy nothing day'. They see most corporate advertising as propaganda and enjoy themselves by subverting it.

www.antiapathy.org – because waking up is hard to do, work out your own twelve-step recovery programme from life-crushing and environmentally destructive conspicuous consumption.

www.authentichappiness.sas.upenn.edu – have fun finding out about yourself with a range of questionnaires and surveys on this site designed by experts in positive psychology.

www.bigbarn.co.uk – BigBarn is a website that enables people to find good food from their nearest local sources.

www.climatespace.org – somewhere to go to share information on what to do about climate change, and much more besides.

www.happyplanetindex.org – to find out what you can do to reduce your environmental impact and to increase your well-being.

www.interdependenceday.co.uk – links to past and future Interdependence Day events, broadcasts and podcasts and to publications and other resources.

www.neweconomics.org – for information about well-being, climate change, the environment and international development.

www.oneworld.net – a wonderful source of news, facts and background information about what is really going on in the world.

www.open.ac.uk – a pioneering provider of interdisciplinary environment and development courses from introductory to postgraduate level.

www.seat61.com – *The Man in Seat Sixty-one* is a website to find out how to travel comfortably by train or ship for many international journeys where you might have thought air was the only option.

www.rivercottage.net – a website about food, where it comes from, and why that matters. Set up by the cook Hugh Fearnley-Whittingstall.

Useful Organizations

Common Ground
www.commonground.org.uk
Gold Hill House, 21 High Street, Shaftesbury, Dorset, SP7 8JE.
+44 (0)1747 850820

Common Ground plays a unique role linking the arts and environmental fields with a focus on celebrating nature and culture.

The Fairtrade Foundation
www.fairtrade.org.uk
Room 204, 16 Baldwin's Gardens, London, EC1N 7RJ
+44 (0)20 7405 5942

The Foundation promotes certified, fairly-traded products and is the UK member of Fairtrade Labelling Organisations International (FLO), which unites twenty national initiatives across Europe, Japan, North America, Mexico and Australia/New Zealand.

Friends of the Earth
www.foe.co.uk
26–28 Underwood Street, London, N1 7JQ
+44 (0)20 7490 1555

The largest international network of environmental groups in the world, represented in fifty-eight countries.

National Consumer Council
www.ncc.org.uk
20 Grosvenor Gardens, London, SW1W 0DH
+44 (0)20 7730 3469

The NCC works in the UK with public service providers, businesses and regulators, and the Government, its main funder, to protect the interests of consumers.

Soil Association
www.soilassociation.org
Bristol House, 40–56 Victoria Street, Bristol, BS1 6BY
 +44 (0)117 929 0661

The UK's leading campaigning and certification body for organic food and farming. It develops and provides practical and sustainable solutions which combine food production and environmental protection and human health.

Slow Food UK
www.slowfood.org.uk
Unit 3, Alliance Court, Eco Park Road, Ludlow, Shropshire, SY8 1FB
+44 (0)1584 879599)

Since the 1980s, Slow Food has become an international organisation of 80,000 members in 90 countries who not only care about enjoying and retaining our diverse heritage of regional food and drink, and protecting it from globalisation, but are increasingly aware of the associated environmental issues.

Scientists for Global Responsibility
www.sgr.org.uk
Ingles Manor, Castle Hill Avenue, Folkestone, Kent, CT20 2RD
+44 (0)1303 851965

An independent UK-based membership organisation of natural and social scientists, engineers, IT professionals and architects. The organisation's principles include openness, accountability, peace, social justice and environmental sustainability. It carries out research, education, and lobbying centred around the military, environmental and political aspects of science, design and technology. The organisation also provides a support network for ethically-concerned professionals in these fields.

The Transition Towns Network
www.transitiontowns.org

Transition Towns is a model and informal network for communities to respond to the twin challenges of Peak Oil and Climate Change. Co-ordinated through a website, anyone interested in becoming active locally can contact people in towns who are already have a plan and learn from their experiences. The site provides a focal point for towns, villages, cities and localities around the world helping to inspire, inform, support and train communities as they consider, adopt and implement their own Transition Initiative.

The Women's Environmental Network
www.wen.org.uk
PO Box 30626 London E1 1TZ
+44 (0)20 7481 9004

Set up in 1988, the Women's Environmental Network's aims include: empowering women to make positive environmental change; increasing awareness of women's perspectives on environmental issues and influencing decision-making to achieve environmental justice for women.

The Women's Institute (WI)
www.womens-institute.org.uk
104 New Kings Road, London, SW6 4LY
+44 (0)20 7371 9300

The WI has campaigned for better food and farming since its inception in 1915. It calls on people who are 'concerned about the power the major supermarkets are having over small independent businesses and farmers both at home and abroad' to 'take action'.

Authors' Biographies

Editors

Andrew Simms is Policy Director and head of the climate change programme at nef, an award-winning UK think-and-do tank, and the author of two other books: *Tescopoly: How One Shop Came out on Top and Why it Matters* (Constable & Robinson, 2007), and *Ecological Debt:The Health of the Planet and the Wealth of Nations* (Pluto, 2005). He studied at the London School of Economics and for several years worked for international development charities such as Oxfam and Christian Aid. He was one of the original campaigners for the Jubilee 2000 debt relief movement. His other work includes publications on climate change, economic globalization and localization, and international development issues including debt, trade, corporate accountability and tackling hunger. He is a board member of Greenpeace UK and The Energy and Resources Institute (TERI) Europe.

Joe Smith is Senior Lecturer in Environment at the Open University. He is author of *What Do Greens Believe?* (Granta, 2006); *Climate Change: from Science to Sustainability* (with Stephen Peake, The Open University, 2003) and *The Daily Globe: Environmental Change, the Public and the Media* (Earthscan, 2000). Joe runs the Cambridge Media and Environment Programme which, since 1996, has run seminars on environmental change and development issues for senior media decision makers, mainly from BBC News and

TV. He has acted as academic consultant on a number of BBC projects including programmes by David Attenborough. Joe initiated the Interdependence Day Project, a new communications and research project, including a collaboration between the OU and nef, that takes a fresh look at global issues. Joe holds a BA degree in Social and Political Sciences and a PhD in Geography from the University of Cambridge.

Contributors

Stephen Bayley

Stephen Bayley was born in Cardiff in 1951 and educated at Manchester University and Liverpool School of Architecture. He is currently architecture and design correspondent of the *Observer* and makes regular contributions as an outspoken commentator on art and design in broadcast and print media. In the eighties he created the successful Boilerhouse Project at the Victoria & Albert Museum and the influential Design Museum which evolved from it. His books include *In Good Shape* (Van Nostrand Reinhold, 1979), *The Albert Memorial* (Scolar Press, 1981), *Harley Earl and the Dream Machine* (Weidenfeld & Nicolson, 1983), *The Conran Directory of Design* (Octopus Conran, 1985), *Sex, Drink and Fast Cars* (Faber & Faber,1986), *Commerce and Culture* (Design Museum, 1989), *Taste* (Faber & Faber, 1991), *Labour Camp* (Batsford, 1998), *General Knowledge* (Booth-Clibborn, 2000), *Sex* (Cassell, 2001), *A Dictionary of Idiocy* (Gibson Square, 2003), *Life's a Pitch* (Bantam, 2007) and *Design: Intelligence Made Visible* (Conran Octopus, 2007). He is married to Flo Bayley, the illustrator and graphic designer, and lives in London with – from time to time – their two children, Bruno (21) and Coco (20).

The Right Honourable Hilary Benn MP

Hilary Benn is MP for Leeds Central and the Secretary of State for Environment, Food and Rural Affairs. The Labour Party has always been in Hilary's life. In 1982, at the age of 29, he was selected as Labour prospective parliamentary candidate for the constituency of Ealing North, which he contested in the 1983 and 1987 General Elections. He then went to work at Manufacturing, Science, Finance – Britain's fifth largest trade union – and represented MSF on the Labour Party's National Policy Forum. From 1994 to 1999, he was Chair of the Management Committee of Unions 21 – the trade union think tank. Following Labour's 1997 General Election victory, he was appointed as special advisor to the Rt Hon. David Blunkett MP, then Secretary of State for Education and Employment. In June 1999, he was elected as Member of Parliament for Leeds Central, and in October 2003 was made Secretary of State for International Development. Following the cabinet reshuffle in June 2007, Hilary was appointed to his present position. When not working, Hilary enjoys gardening and watching sport. He is married and has four children.

John Bird

John Bird was a poor boy, orphan, thief, inmate, artist and poet before going on to found the ground-breaking social initiative that is *The Big Issue*. Since setting up *The Big Issue* magazine and foundation to help the homeless help themselves, John has become an authority on motivation. He has spoken at the UN in New York, Nairobi and Istanbul and at Downing Street and Buckingham Palace. The UN Scroll of Honour, an MBE and the 2005/6 Beacon Prize for Creative Giving are three of many accolades and awards he has received. Since the inception of *The Big Issue* in 1991, he has overseen its development to become the UK's most successful social enterprise, stretching from Tokyo to Totnes. John's latest venture is called Wedge Card, a loyalty card aimed at revitalizing the local high street. He has written an autobiography *Some Luck* (Penguin, 2002) and the bestselling *How to Change your Life in 7 Steps* (Vermilion, 2007). Now aged 61, he has recently remarried for the third time and he has five children. John is also standing as an independent candidate in the Mayor of London election in 2008.

Rosie Boycott

Rosie Boycott is a writer and broadcaster appearing regularly on radio and TV programmes including BBC Radio 4's *Start the Week*, *Question Time*, *Any Questions*, *The Late Review* and various other talk shows and arts programmes. Rosie is a member of and media advisor for the Council of Europe, a director of the Hay-on-Wye Literary Festival and is also involved with Warchild and StreetSmart. Rosie was a founder of *Spare Rib* magazine and Virago Press and was the first woman to edit a broadsheet and daily newspaper. She has edited *Esquire*, the *Independent on Sunday*, the *Independent* and the *Daily* and *Sunday Express*. She has also contributed to and edited newspapers and magazines in Kuwait, Hong Kong and the USA. Her books include *Batty Bloomers and Boycott* (Hutchinson, 1982), *A Nice Girl Like Me* (her autobiography, Chatto & Windus, 1984), *All For Love* (Chatto & Windus, 1988), a novel, and most recently, *Our Farm* (Bloomsbury, 2007).

David Boyle

David Boyle is a fellow of nef, the author of *Authenticity: Brands, Fakes, Spin and the Lust for Real Life* (HarperCollins, 2004) and of a number of books including *Blondel's Song: The Imprisonment and Ransom of Richard the Lionheart* (Penguin,

2005) and *The Tyranny of Numbers* (HarperCollins, 2001). His book *Funny Money* (HarperCollins, 1999) launched the time banks movement in the UK. His work on the future of money includes *Why London Needs its own Currency* (nef, 2000), *Virtual Currencies* (Financial Times, 2000), *The Money Changers: Currency reform from Aristotle to e-cash* (Earthscan, 2002) and *The Little Money Book* (Alastair Sawday, 2003). He has written for many national newspapers and magazines, and edited a range of magazines including *Town & Country Planning* and *Liberal Democrat News*. He is the editor of *Radical Economics*. He lives in Crystal Palace, in south London, with his wife Sarah and sons Robin and William.

The Right Honourable David Cameron MP, Leader of the Opposition

David was first elected as the Conservative Member of Parliament for the Witney constituency in west Oxfordshire in June 2001. He was a member of the Home Affairs Select Committee and took an interest in a wide range of subjects. He has previously held the positions of Shadow Deputy Leader of the House of Commons (2003), Deputy Chairman of the Conservative Party (2003), Front Bench spokesman on Local Government Finance (2004) and Head of Policy Co-ordination up until May 2005. After the general election in 2005, David held the position of Shadow Secretary of State for Education and Skills. In December 2005 he became the Leader of HM Opposition. Born in October 1966, David has worked at a high level in both business and Government. He spent almost seven years at Carlton Communications plc, one of the UK's leading media companies, where he was Director of Corporate Affairs and served on the Executive Board. David is married to Samantha and has three children. Outside work, David's interests include playing tennis, riding, country sports and watching television. He is a keen cook.

Larry Elliott

Larry Elliott has been a financial journalist for more than twenty years and has been economics editor of the *Guardian* since 1994. He was educated at Cambridge University and has worked for newspapers since 1978. He lives in Hertfordshire with his wife and two children. He is a trustee of the Scott Trust, which owns the *Guardian*; a council member of the Overseas Development Institute; a Justice of the Peace and a visiting fellow at the University of Hertfordshire. With Dan Atkinson, he wrote *The Age of Insecurity* (Verso, 1998).

Hugh Fearnley-Whittingstall

Hugh Fearnley-Whittingstall lives in Dorset with his wife Marie and their children, Oscar, Freddie and Chloe. A talented writer, broadcaster and campaigner, Hugh is widely known for his commitment to seasonal, ethically produced food and has earned a huge following through his *River Cottage* television series and books. He started living in the original River Cottage in rural Dorset in 1998, determined to start growing and rearing some of his own food. His steep learning curve was documented in the *Escape to River Cottage* series on Channel 4. Ten years on, he and his team are based at River Cottage HQ, a working farm on the Devon-Dorset border, from where they run a broad range of events and courses. Hugh's latest project involves opening the River Cottage Local Produce Store and Canteen, with the most recent of the series of River Cottage books, *The River Cottage Fish Book*, published in late 2007. He is patron of the National Farmers' Retail and Markets Association (FARMA). Hugh also writes a weekly column in the *Guardian*.

Professor A.C. Grayling

Anthony Grayling MA, DPhil (Oxon) FRSL, FRSA is Professor of Philosophy at Birkbeck College, University of London, and a Supernumerary Fellow of St Anne's College, Oxford. He has written and edited many books on philosophy and other subjects; among his most recent are a biography of William Hazlitt (Weidenfeld & Nicolson, 2000) and a collection of essays. For several years he wrote the 'Last Word' column for the *Guardian* newspaper and he is a regular reviewer for the *Literary Review* and the *Financial Times*. He also often writes for the *Observer, Economist, Times Literary Supplement, Independent on Sunday* and *New Statesman*, and is a frequent broadcaster on the BBC. He is the Editor of *Online Review London* and Contributing Editor of *Prospect* magazine. He is a past chairman of June Fourth, a human rights group concerned with China. He is a Fellow of the Royal Society of Literature and also a Fellow of the Royal Society of Arts, and in 2003 was a Booker Prize judge.

David Goldblatt

David Goldblatt is a writer, broadcaster and teacher. His most recent book is *The Ball is Round: A Global History of Football* (Viking, 2006).

Wayne Hemingway

Wayne Hemingway was born in 1961 in Morecambe. His earliest memories are of his mum and Nan dressing him up as Elvis, a Beatle or Tarzan. After spending most of his childhood in Blackburn, Wayne went on to gain a degree in geography and town planning at University College, London.

After selling the contents of his and wife Geraldine's wardrobe at Camden Market, Wayne realized that money could be made from fashion. Together they built Red or Dead into a label that received global acclaim, winning the prestigious British Fashion Council's Street Style Designer of the Year Award for an unprecedented three consecutive years from 1996. In 1999, having sold Red or Dead, they set up Hemingway Design, specializing in affordable and social design, which has won a number of high profile awards. Wayne is the Chairman of Building for Life, a CABE-funded organization that promotes excellence in the quality of design of new housing. His latest business is a design resource *The Land of Lost Content*, www.lolc.co.uk Wayne maintains his ability to balance a hectic lifestyle with being a passionate father of four. He also loves Blackburn Rovers.

Tom Hodgkinson

Tom Hodgkinson is editor of *The Idler* and author of *How To Be Idle* (HarperCollins, 2005) and *How To Be Free* (Penguin, 2007). He was educated at Westminster School, Jesus College, Cambridge and Slam City Skates, London. He founded *The Idler* in 1993 after a disillusioning flirtation with the world of the nine-to-five. Following a stint at the *Guardian*'s special projects department, he worked on magazines for various clients including Channel 4 and Sony Playstation. Five years ago he and his partner and children moved out of Shepherds Bush to a farmhouse in north Devon where they are attempting to fatten pigs, grow vegetables, drink large quantities of alcohol, throw feasts and parties and generally get medieval. He is currently learning to play the ukulele.

Oliver James

Oliver James is the author of *They F*** You Up – How to Survive Family Life* (Bloomsbury, 2002) and *Affluenza – How to be Successful and Stay Sane* (Vermilion, 2007). He has also written *Britain on the Couch – Why are We Unhappier than We Were in the 1950s – Despite being Richer* (Century, 1997) and *Juvenile Violence in a Winner-Loser Culture* (Free Association, 1995). He is a regular broadcaster in the British media and has contributed articles to scientific journals in recent years, including the *Journal of Epidemiology and Community Health* and *The Psychologist*. Oliver has acted as an advisor to both New Labour and the Conservative parties.

Caroline Lucas MEP

Caroline is a former Principal Speaker for the Green Party and was elected as one of the Green Party's first MEPs in 1999 and re-elected in 2004 for a second term. A member of the Committee on the Environment, Public Health and Food Safety, her work has included amending legislation to strengthen the case against GM crops, pushing for stricter controls on the regulation of chemicals, and promoting more ambitious targets on CO_2 emissions to combat climate change. Caroline is also a member of the Committee on International Trade, and Co-founder and Co-President of the cross-party group on peace initiatives. She serves as Vice President of Stop the War Coalition; CND National Council Member; Board member of the International Forum on Globalization; Matron of the Women's Environmental Network; Vice-President of the RSPCA; and Patron of Action for UN Renewal. In 2006 she was included in the Environment Agency's Top 100 Eco-Heroes of all time, and earlier this year was voted the *Observer*'s Politician of the Year.

Nic Marks

Nic Marks is founder of the Centre for Well-Being at nef and has led the well-being programme there since 2001. Nic is a recognized expert in the field of well-being research and undertakes innovative research in the use of well-being indicators in public policy environments. He was the co-author of nef's innovative *Happy Planet Index,* a global index of human well-being and environmental impact. He is an advisor to the government of Bhutan, working with the Centre for Bhutanese Studies on how to construct indicators for assessing Gross National Happiness (GNH).

Kevin McCloud

Kevin is best known for Channel 4's *Grand Designs* and for his annual coverage of the Stirling Prize for architecture each October. He also presented *Demolition* for Channel 4 in 2005 (with a follow-up in 2006) in which he, George Ferguson and Janet Street-Porter started a campaign to improve public space in our towns and cities. A major series about urban regeneration built on that in 2007. He admits to having had an unhealthy obsession for buildings since childhood: he studied them, has designed everything in and around them, has lit them and written about them. He now has a column in the *Sunday Times* in which he takes on planners, architects and developers and also writes for *Grand Designs* magazine. His two ambitions are to entertain and to make the built environment better – and consequently 'make people feel better'. His favourite colour is Yves Klein blue.

Ann Pettifor

In the 1990s Ann Pettifor helped design and lead a groundbreaking international campaign, Jubilee 2000, which succeeded in persuading large swathes of world public opinion, as well as world leaders, that much of the debt of forty-two poor countries should be cancelled. Ann has served on the board of the UN's Human Development Report in 2002 and 2003; and as a member of the high level group of the Helsinki Process on globalization, sponsored by the Tanzanian and Finnish governments. She is the author of *The Coming First World Debt Crisis* (Palgrave Macmillan, 2006) and editor of nef's *Real World Economic Outlook* (2003). She has an honorary doctorate from the University of Newcastle; was awarded the Freedom of the City of Callao in Peru in 1999; the 2000 Pax Christi International Peace Prize; and was made a member of the Order of the Niger by President Obasanjo in 2002. She currently leads an international advocacy consultancy, Advocacy International Ltd, which advised the Nigerian government on its $18 billion debt cancellation strategy in 2005.

Philip Pullman

Philip was born in Norwich in 1946, and educated in England, Zimbabwe, and Australia, before settling with his parents in north Wales. He went to Exeter College, Oxford, to read English, and spent many years in the teaching profession. He maintains a passionate interest in education, having voiced concerns that an over-emphasis on testing and league tables has led to a lack of time and freedom for a true, imaginative and humane engagement with literature. Philip is the author of nearly twenty books. His most well-known work is the trilogy *His Dark Materials*. These books have been honoured by several prizes, including the Carnegie Medal, the *Guardian* Children's Book Award, and (for *The Amber Spyglass*) the Whitbread Book of the Year Award – the first time in the history of that prize that it was given to a children's book. When not writing books Philip likes to draw, make things out of wood and attempt to play the piano. http://www.philip-pullman.com.

Anita Roddick

Anita started The Body Shop in 1976 to create a livelihood for herself and her two daughters, while her husband, Gordon, was trekking across the Americas. She started without any training or experience and only Gordon's advice to take sales to £300 a week. Now, thirty years on, The Body Shop is a multi-local business with over 2,045 stores serving over 77 million customers in 51 different markets in 25 different languages and across 12 time zones. The Body Shop was sold to L'Oréal in 2006 and Anita remained as a consultant until her death in September 2007. On what would have been her 65th birthday, a website and day of activism was launched that aims to continue Anita's work, www.iamanactivist.org.

Colin Tudge

Colin Tudge was educated as a biologist and has special interests in natural history, evolution and genetics, food and farming, politics, and the relationship between science and religion. He has earned his living this past forty years or so by writing with occasional forays into broadcasting. His many books include *The Variety of Life* (Oxford University Press, 2000), *So Shall We Reap* (Allen Lane, 2003), *The Secret Life of Trees* (Allen Lane, 2005) and – most recently – *Feeding People is Easy* (Pari Publishing, 2007). He nurses the conviction that human beings are basically both sensible and nice and that if only democracy could be made to work then the world would be a much better place.

Adair Turner

Adair Turner has combined careers in business, public policy and academia. He is currently Vice-Chairman of Merrill Lynch Europe, a director of United Business Media plc, chair of the UK Low Pay Commission and chair of the UK Pensions Commission. Adair is also a visiting professor at the London School of Economics and CASS Business School, City of London and an independent cross-bench peer in the House of Lords. After studying history and economics at Cambridge University, Adair taught economics part-time in parallel with his business career. He worked for British Petroleum and Chase Manhattan Bank before joining McKinsey & Company in 1982, becoming a director in 1994. From 1995 to 1999 he was Director-General of the Confederation of British Industry. Adair is a trustee of the World Wide Fund for Nature and a member of the Council of Management of the National Institute of Economic and Social Research (NIESR). He is the author of *Just Capital – The Liberal Economy* (Macmillan, 2001).